VISIT VERSAILLES

versailles

This book is published and edited
jointly by Artlys and the Château de Versailles.

Artlys editorial director: Denis Kilian
Editorial coordination: Karine Barou
Graphic design and production: Martine Mène
Plans: Thierry Lebreton, Dominique Bissière
Computer-assisted publishing: Hervé Delemotte
Production director: Pierre Kegels

ISBN 978-2-85495-293-3

VISIT VERSAILLES

versailles

BÉATRIX SAULE
Head curator,
director of the Château de Versailles research centre

Historic introduction
by Pierre Arizzoli-Clémentel,
Director General of the Château de Versailles

CHÂTEAU DE VERSAILLES

art lys musées et monuments

CONTENTS

WALKS IN THE GARDENS

VERSAILLES

Louis XIII (1601-1643) — Anne of Austria (1601-1666)

1624
Louis XIII has a hunting lodge built at Versailles.

1631
Louis XIII asks Philibert Le Roy to build a château on the site of the hunting lodge.

1643
Louis XIII stays at Versailles for the last time.

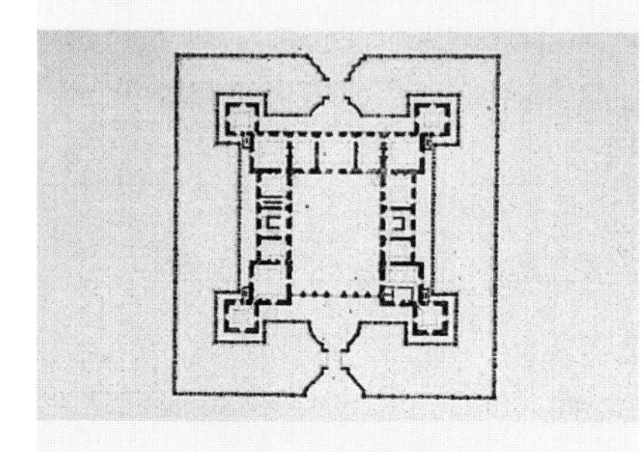

Louis XIII's "little château"

Louis XIV (1638-1715) — Maria Theresa of Austria (1638-1683)

1660
Marriage of Louis XIV to Maria Theresa of Austria. The King brings his wife to Versailles on October 25.

1664
Festivities of Les Plaisirs de l'île enchantée.

1668
Grand Divertissement at Versailles.

1682
Louis XIV declares Versailles the official residence of the Court and seat of government.

Pierre Patel, *The Château of Versailles in 1668*

- Louis, Dauphin (1661-1711)
  - Louis, duc de Bourgogne (1682-1712)
  - Philippe, duc d'Anjou, became Philip V of Spain in 1700 (1683-1746)
  - Charles, duc de Berry (1686-1714)
- Louis-François (1672-1672)
- Philippe-Charles (1668-1671)
- Marie-Thérèse (1667-1672)
- Marie-Anne (1664-1664)
- Anne-Elisabeth (1662-1662)

1684
Completion of the Hall of Mirrors.

1710
Consecration of the Chapel Royal on June 5.

1715
September 1, death of Louis XIV. September 9, Louis XV abandons Versailles for Vincennes.

The colonnade (construction started in 1685) by Jules Hardouin-Mansart

ENGLAND AND THE USA

1625
Charles I is proclaimed King of England.

1649
Charles I is beheaded.

1653
Oliver Cromwell is proclaimed Lord Protector.

1658
Death of Cromwell. The Monarchy is restored.

1660
Charles II crowned king of England.

1666
Fire of London.

1682
The Sieur de la Salle founds Louisiana.

1688
James II escapes to France.

1713
Treaty of Utrecht, Spanish possessions are divided: Philip V, grandson of Louis XIV, keeps Spain and its colonies, Britain gains Gibraltar, Minorca, Newfoundland, Nova Scotia, and the Hudson Bay territories.

1714-1727
Reign of George I.

Louis XV (1710-1774) — Maria Leszczinska (1703-1768)

1722
Louis XV returns to live at Versailles.

1736
September 26, opening of the Hercules Salon.

1757
Attempt on Louis XV's life by Damiens.

1768
The Petit Trianon is completed.

1774
May 10, Louis XV dies of smallpox at Versailles.

Pierre-Denis Martin, *Château of Versailles in 1722*

- Louis Dauphin (1729-1765)
- Philippe-Louis (1730-1733)
- Adélaïde (1732-1800)
- Victoire (1733-1799)
- Sophie (1734-1782)
- Thérèse-Félicité (1736-1744)
- Louise (1737-1787)

Louis XVI (1754-1793) — Marie-Antoinette of Austria-Lorraine (1755-1793)

1777
Visit of Joseph II, Emperor of Austria, the Queen's brother.

1783
Signing of the Treaty of Versailles, acknowledging the independence of the United States of America.

1783-1786
Construction of the Queen's Hamlet.

1789
May 5, opening of the States General.
October 6, the King, the Royal Family and the Court leave Versailles for good.

Claude-Louis Châtelet, *Illumination of the Belvedere in honour of Joseph II*

Louis-Philippe (1773-1850)

1837
June 10, Louis-Philippe inaugurates the museum dedicated to the glories of France.

Jean-Augusta Bard, *Inauguration of the Battle Gallery*

1688
James II escapes to France.

1713
Treaty of Utrecht, Spanish possessions are divided:
Philip V, grandson of Louis XIV, keeps Spain and its colonies,
Britain gains Gibraltar, Minorca, Newfoundland, Nova Scotia, and the Hudson Bay territories.

1714-1727
Reign of George I.

1787
September 17, United States Constitution.

1788
Creation of The Times.

1789
George Washington elected President of the United States of America.

1837
Queen Victoria rises to the throne.

WALKS IN THE GARDENS

WEST SIDE

1 The Parterre d'Eau or Water Parterre
2 The Latona Parterre and Basin
3 The Royal Avenue or Green Carpet
4 The Apollo Basin
5 The Grand Canal

NORTH SIDE

6 The Parterre du Nord or North Flowerbed
7 The Pyramid Fountain
8 The Fountain of Nymphs' Basin
9 The Water Avenue
10 The Dragon Basin
11 The Neptune Basin

SOUTH SIDE

12 The Parterre du Midi or South Flowerbed
13 The Orangery
14 The Swiss Pool

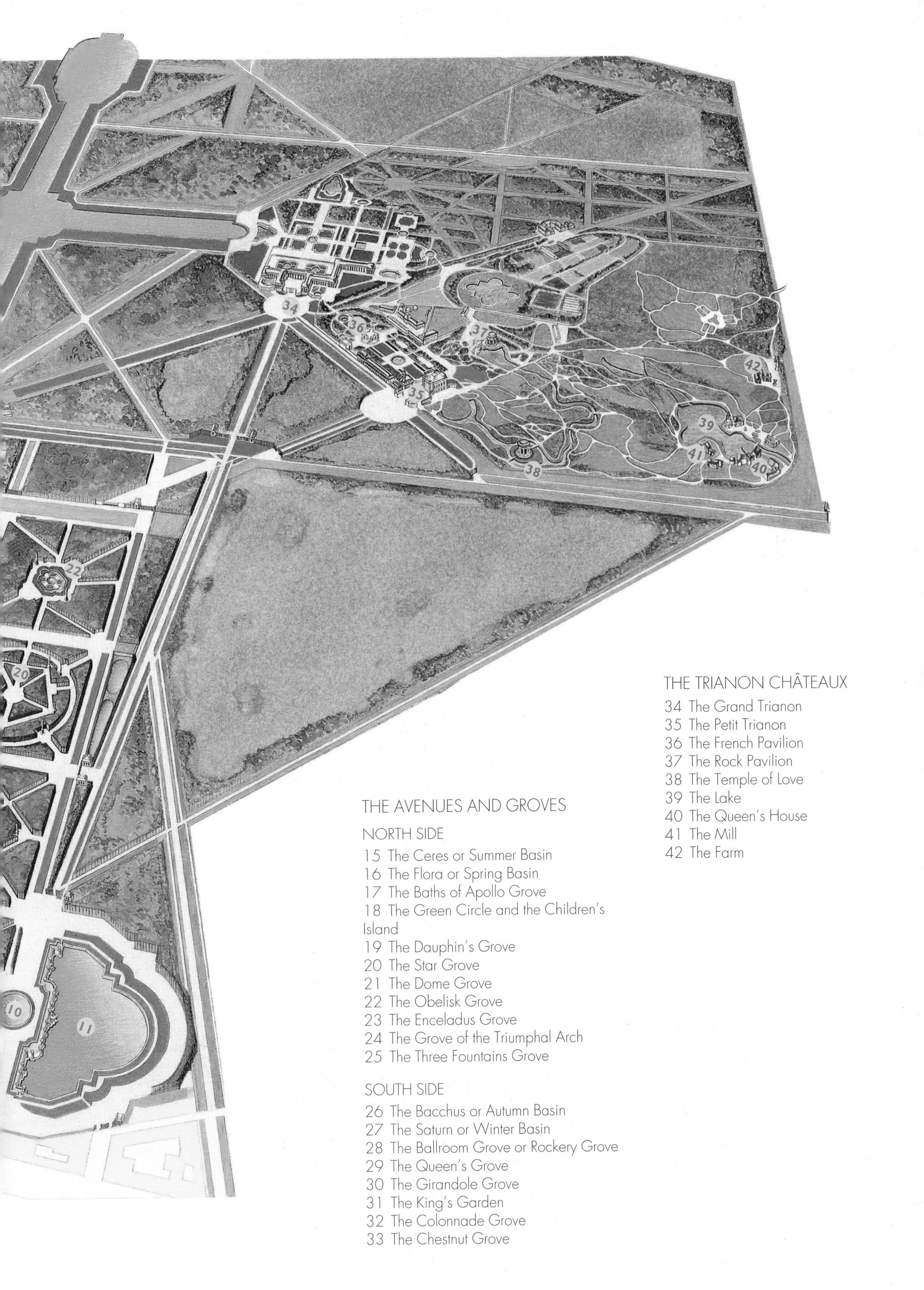
THE AVENUES AND GROVES
NORTH SIDE
15 The Ceres or Summer Basin
16 The Flora or Spring Basin
17 The Baths of Apollo Grove
18 The Green Circle and the Children's Island
19 The Dauphin's Grove
20 The Star Grove
21 The Dome Grove
22 The Obelisk Grove
23 The Enceladus Grove
24 The Grove of the Triumphal Arch
25 The Three Fountains Grove
SOUTH SIDE
26 The Bacchus or Autumn Basin
27 The Saturn or Winter Basin
28 The Ballroom Grove or Rockery Grove
29 The Queen's Grove
30 The Girandole Grove
31 The King's Garden
32 The Colonnade Grove
33 The Chestnut Grove
THE TRIANON CHÂTEAUX
34 The Grand Trianon
35 The Petit Trianon
36 The French Pavilion
37 The Rock Pavilion
38 The Temple of Love
39 The Lake
40 The Queen's House
41 The Mill
42 The Farm

GROUND FLOOR OF THE CHÂTEAU

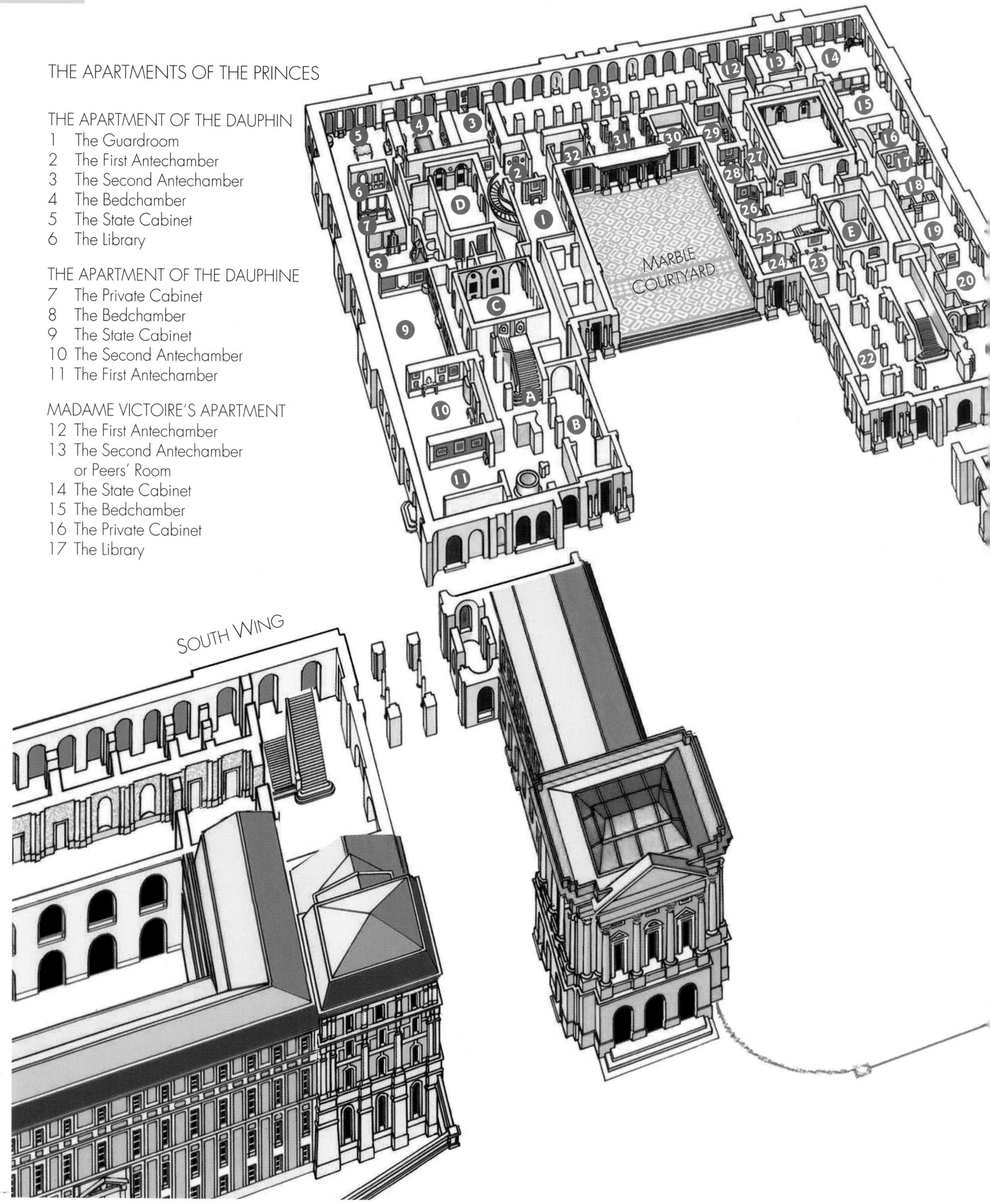

MADAME ADELAIDE'S APARTMENT
18 The Private Cabinet
19 The Bedchamber
20 The State Cabinet
21 The Archers' Room
22 The Vestibule to the former Ambassadors' Staircase
23 The Vestibule
24 The Guardroom
25 The King's Staircase

THE CAPTAIN OF THE GUARD'S APARTMENT
26 The State Cabinet
27 The Private Cabinet
28 The Bedchamber

MARIE-ANTOINETTE'S APARTMENT
29 The Queen's Service Room
30 The Bedchamber
31 The Marble Vestibule
32 The Bathroom
33 The Lower Gallery

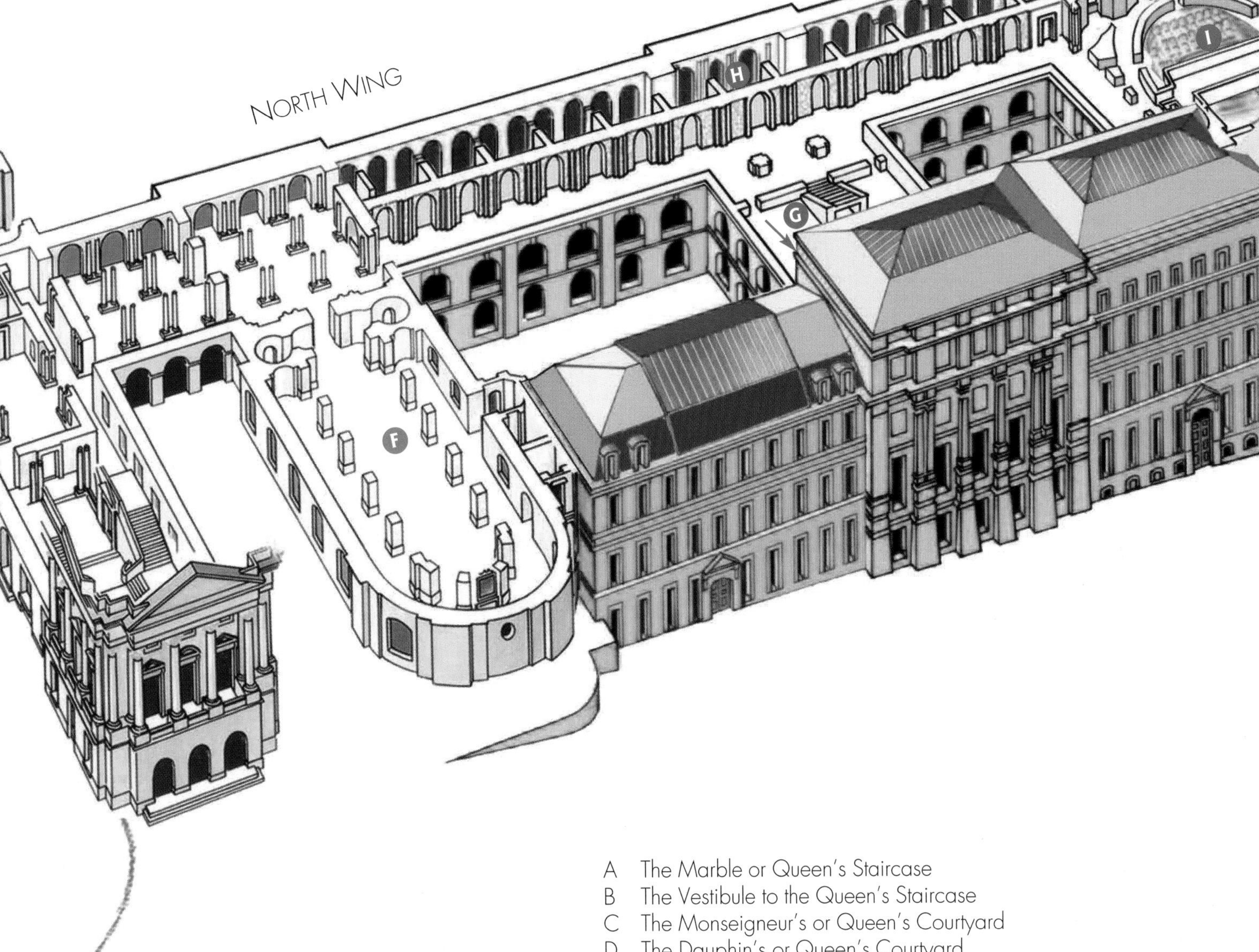

A The Marble or Queen's Staircase
B The Vestibule to the Queen's Staircase
C The Monseigneur's or Queen's Courtyard
D The Dauphin's or Queen's Courtyard
E The King's Private Courtyard
F The Chapel Royal
G The Crusades Room
H The 17th Century Rooms
I The Opera

FIRST FLOOR OF THE CHÂTEAU

THE STATE APARTMENTS

THE KING'S GRAND APARTMENT

1 The Hercules Salon
2 The Abundance Salon
3 The Venus Salon
4 The Diana Salon
5 The Mars Salon
6 The Mercury Salon
7 The Apollo Salon

THE HALL OF MIRRORS AND ITS SALONS

8 The Salon of War
9 The Hall of Mirrors
10 The Salon of Peace

THE QUEEN'S SUITE

11 The Queen's Bedchamber
12 The Peers' Salon
13 The Antechamber for Grand Couvert repasts
14 The Queen's Guards Room

THE CORONATION ROOM

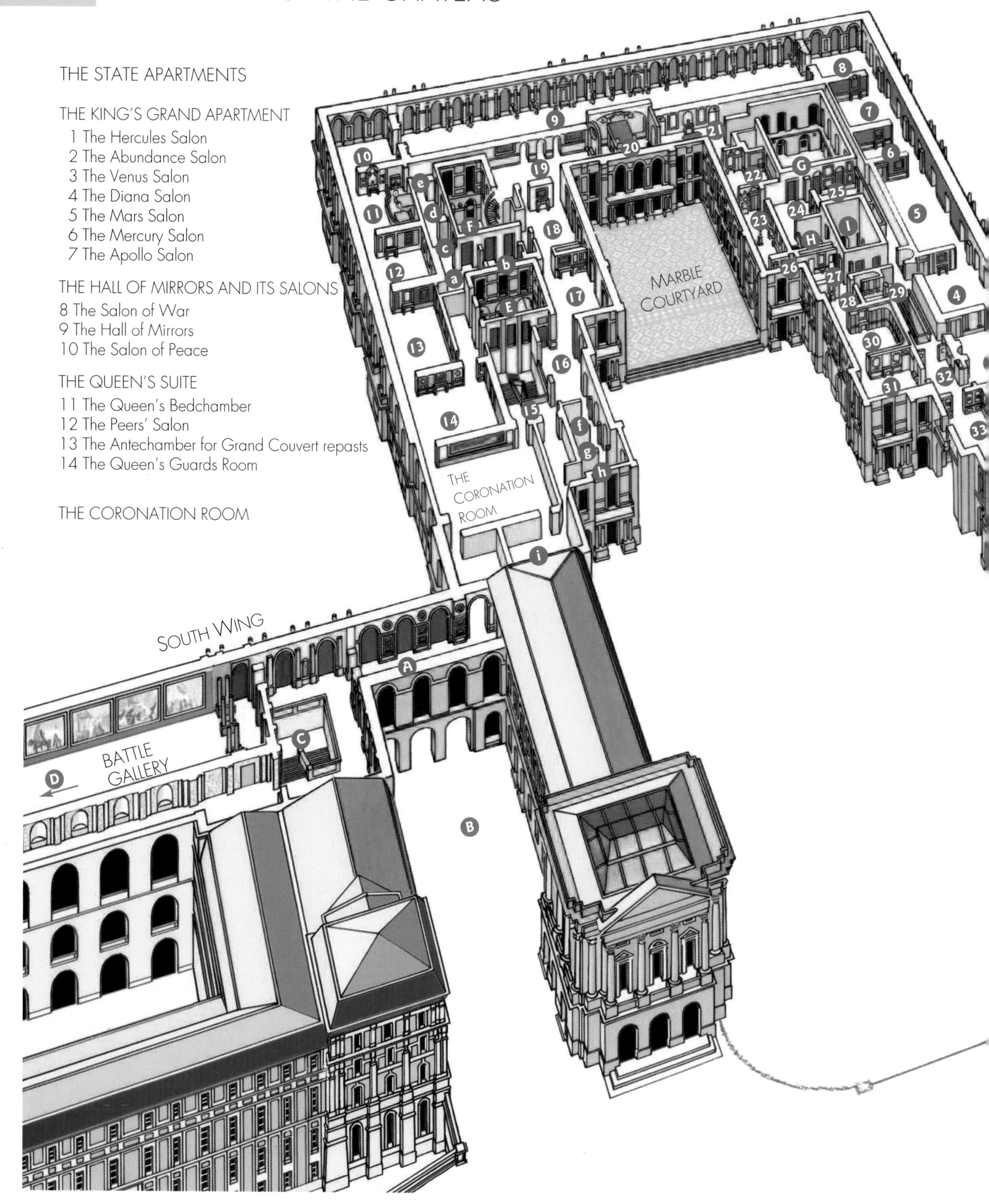

THE PRIVATE APARTMENTS

MARIE-ANTOINETTE'S PRIVATE APARTMENTS
a The Library Annex
b The Gilded Study
c The Library
d The Meridian Cabinet
e The Duchess of Burgundy's Cabinet

MADAME DE MAINTENON'S APARTMENTS
f and g The Antechambers
h The Bedchamber
i The State Cabinet

THE KING'S APARTMENTS
15 The Marble (or Queen's) Staircase
16 The loggia also giving access to the King's apartment
17 The King's Guards Room
18 The First Antechamber
19 The Œil-de-Bœuf Salon
20 The King's Bedchamber
21 The Council Cabinet

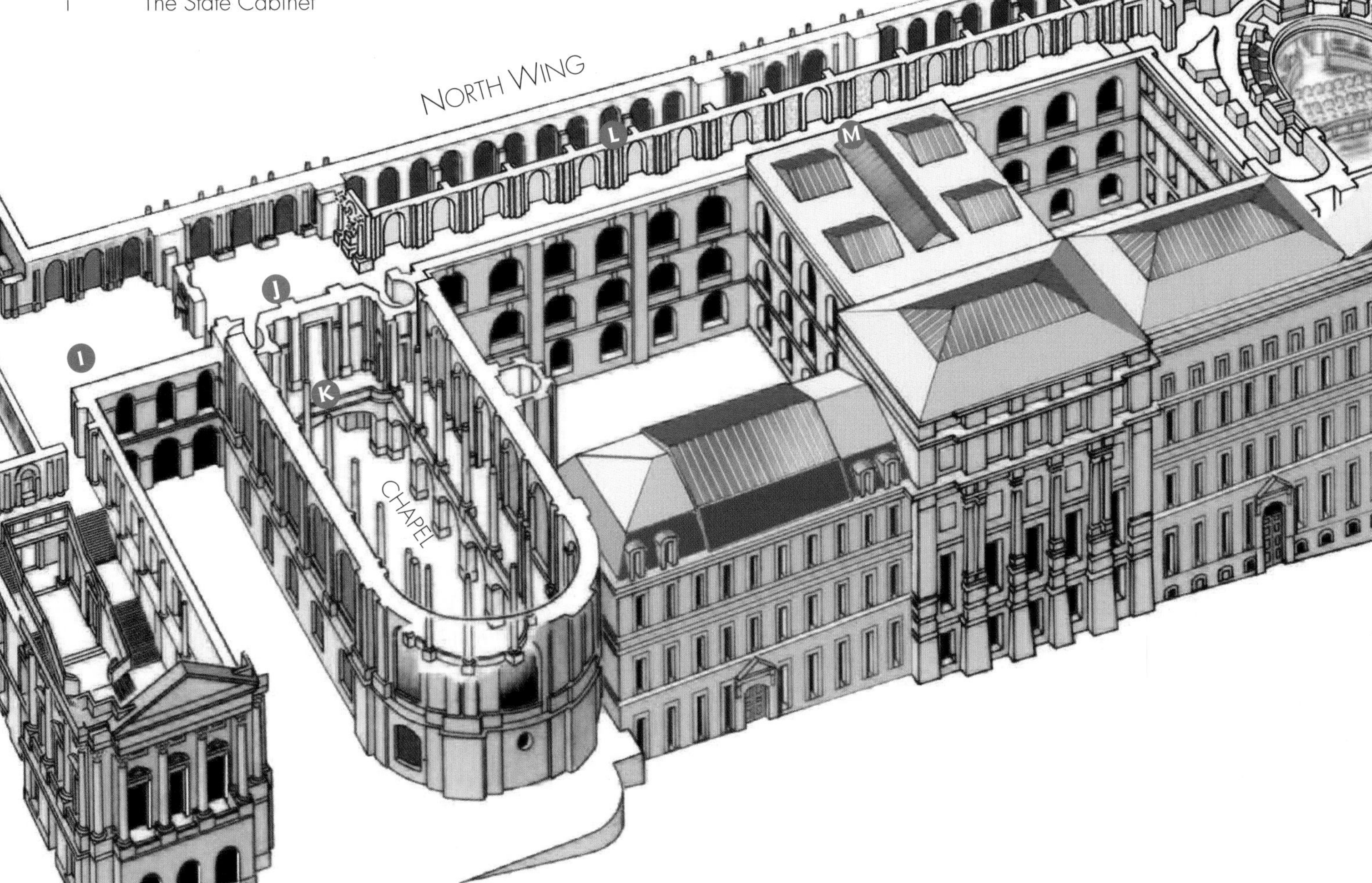

THE KING'S PRIVATE APARTMENTS
22 Louis XV's Bedchamber
23 The Clock Cabinet
24 The Dogs' Antechamber
25 The Post-Hunt Dining Room
26 The Inner Cabinet or Corner Cabinet
27 The Dispatch Cabinet
28 The Golden Dishes Room
29 The Bathroom
30 Louis XVI's Library
31 The Porcelain Dining Room
32 The Buffet Room
33 Louis XVI's Games Room

A The Merchants' Room or 1792 room
B The Princes' Courtyard
C The Princes' Staircase
D The 1830 Room
E The Monseigneur's or Queen's Courtyard
F The Dauphin's or Queen's Courtyard
G The Stags' Courtyard
H The King's Staircase
I The King's Private Staircase
J The Chapel Salon
K The Royal Tribune of the Chapel
L The 17th Century Rooms
M The 19th Century Rooms

VERSAILLES, SEAT OF THE OLD MONARCHY

Although Louis XIII had a hunting lodge built with its own gardens on the site in the 1630s, it was really Louis XIV who created Versailles. Removed from the rebellious people of Paris, yet within reach of the city, the site offered plenty of opportunity to build: it thus fulfilled the King's desire to gather his Court around him, something that no other royal residence in the area could offer. It was he who gave the palace its grandeur; it was he who mapped out its destiny. Between 1682 and 1789, Versailles was the seat of the absolute monarchy and became its symbol, since the place itself, modelled according to the Sun King's wishes, reflects the way he conceived power.

THE DWELLING PLACE OF ALL POWER

In an absolute monarchy, all power comes from the King. In Versailles, Louis XIV was Master of his own house, just as he was Master of the kingdom that he governed through intermediaries that owed him everything. Excluded from affairs of government, the Nobility no longer held any real power, yet they nonetheless felt the need to appear at Court. It was there that the King dispensed favours: offices, land, titles, pensions, etc. In this society founded on prestige and appearances, emulation was constant, luxury compulsory, life extravagant. In this way, Louis XIV "had a hold" over his courtiers. It was he who had to dominate in every way; in his eyes, the exercise and outward signs of power were one and the same thing. His residence had to be the biggest and the most beautiful and its décor loaded with symbols to his glory. The number of servants, in the noble sense of the term, assembled in the King's House, had to be the greatest and his Court had to be attended by the most people; between 3000 and 10,000 courtiers, depending on the day. This huge crowd had to be strictly regulated. Etiquette and its constraints – who had access to the King, who had the right to sit down in his presence, who was ranked above whom, etc. – may seem pointless to us today. However, etiquette was essential, since it served to confirm ranks, the primacy of the King, in short the hierarchy within the Court. It applied to the Sovereign's most private moments – getting up in the morning, going to bed at night, mealtimes, going for walks – which were perceived as acts of State when acts of State appeared to be the King's personal acts. Another specific feature of Versailles, and something which naturally astonished foreigners, was that both the gardens and the inside of the Château were largely open to the public. Anyone, be they a member of the Court or otherwise, could see the King when he crossed his State Apartments to go to the Chapel. They could even go right into his Bedchamber, as long as he was not there. All these functions – representation, government, accommodation and service – explain the layout of the place. But it was not built in a day.

FIFTY YEARS OF BUILDING WORK

When Louis XIV came to have fun in his father's manor at the start of his own reign in 1661 and ordered the first alterations, even he could never have imagined that this small building, consisting at the time of the buildings that surround the Marble Courtyard today, was to become the core of a vast complex. During this youthful period, the gardens, immediately entrusted to Le Nôtre, were the setting for festivities so extraordinary that Versailles became known throughout Europe. It was the day after the 1668 party that the King decided on the first extensions. Le Vau and d'Orbay, the King's architects, enveloped the old château with three main buildings overlooking the park. The new buildings, constructed in stone and according to the tastes of the time – a baroque Roman villa style –, contrasted so starkly with the brick, stone and slate architecture dating from the time of Louis XIII, that there appeared to be two châteaux, slotted one into the other. Le Brun, Chief Painter to the King, provided the drawings for all the internal décor of the State Apartments and for the sculptures of the fountains with their multiple water effects in the parterres, avenues and groves. Apollo, the Sun God with whom the King was identified, reigned throughout.
In 1677, Louis XIV announced his decision to move the Court and Government to Versailles permanently. Thus began an immense building project, which, in spite of the tens of thousands of men working on it, was far from complete in 1682 when the King actually moved in. Under the direction of J. Hardouin-Mansart the built-on area was

increased five-fold, with the construction of two stables, the Grand Lodgings, the South and North wings and the Grand Trianon. The Hall of Mirrors replaced the central terrace on the first floor. The interiors were constantly renovated, the groves continuously redesigned, the water pipe work increasingly ambitious. But wars towards the end of the King's reign hampered the progress of the projects. The Chapel was only completed in 1710. It was the King's determination and fifty years of hard work, hesitations, trials and tribulations that ultimately led to the creation of a whole where everything was carefully mastered– both nature and men –, where everything was ordered and structured around a line passing through the centre of the royal residence, where the King's bedchamber had been located since 1701.

OUTWARDLY NOTHING CHANGED

The death of Louis XIV in 1715 did not lead to the end of this court "machinery", which had become an attribute of royalty and Versailles in its own right. Up until 1789, it was imposed on Louis XV then on Louis XVI, who were required to reproduce the same customs in the same places as their forefather. Despite being increasingly seen as restrictive, expensive and antiquated, no reforms could be made without affecting too many privileges. So Versailles continued to function in the same way as it had under the Great King, outwardly at least. Unlike Louis XVI who was not a building king, Louis XV perfected the work of his great-grandfather, with this same spirit of magnificence, commissioning the decoration of the Hercules Salon, the Neptune Basin and the Opera.
But in addition to this ceremonial life, these sovereigns also led a simple personal life, sparing them from the constraints of etiquette. The fashion was for elegance and privacy. Nooks within the château, small apartments and private cabinets multiplied, housing a very small circle of family and friends, in décors constantly updated to reflect the tastes of their time. The greatest sophistication was reflected in the décor, the conversation, the music, the food, etc.
Kings and Queens too frequently withdrew to their own private apartments or to Trianon. Louis XV, and especially Marie-Antoinette, adopted this attitude with no heed for the consequences. The courtiers grew tired of it all, wondering "What's the point of coming to Versailles?" On the eve of the Revolution, the Court was often deserted, the nobility had distanced itself from the King.

FROM THE REVOLUTION TO THE PRESENT DAY

The Revolution emptied the château of its furnishings but spared the building itself. After years of neglect, it was restored first by Napoleon I, and then by Kings Louis XVIII and Charles X, both brothers of Louis XVI. But none dared make it the seat of power: moving into Versailles would constitute provocation; it would be too suggestive of a return to the Ancien Régime and its privileges. For a while, nobody knew what to do with it and demolition was even considered, but the château was ultimately saved by King Louis-Philippe. In a spirit of national reconciliation, the "King of the French" transformed it into a museum, dedicated to "all of France's glories". Opened in 1837, the History Galleries recount a concise story of France's history in monumental form, from the foundation of the kingdom to modern times.
Alongside the History Museum, since the start of the century curators and architects have focused on restoring and refurnishing the royal and princely apartments that make up the core of the château, at the same time adding to the collections of paintings and sculptures that still occupy its wings.
Three centuries after its creation, the estate, despite having lost its hunting grounds, still remains vast, with its three châteaux, its garden, its park and outbuildings: 800 hectares of grounds, 20 km of roads, the same amount of closing walls, 200,000 trees and even more flowers planted every year, 35 km of water pipes, 11 hectares of roofs, 2,153 windows, 67 staircases...

Pierre Arizzoli-Clémentel
Director General of the Château de Versailles

THE COACH MUSEUM

The Coach Museum is located in the Grand Stables built by J. Hardouin-Mansart in 1680. It occupies a gallery that has retained its former appearance, its oak panelling with hay racks and its elegant wrought iron lanterns. The carriages on display were assembled by Louis-Philippe. It was thus that Napoleon Ist's wedding party arrived at Versailles on 2 April 1810 in seven ceremonial coaches evoking the splendour of the imperial court at its height. Also on display is Charles X's coronation carriage, designed by the architect Percier for Louis XVIII, but which the latter never dared use in the political context of the recent Restoration. Louis-Philippe also purchased sedan-chairs and sleighs; the latter were already at Versailles under the Ancien Régime when they were used for racing along the snow-covered paths of the grounds or on the frozen Grand Canal. In 1833, Louis XVIII's funeral carriage joined these vehicles; it is the only remaining example of a royal funeral hearse.

Louis XVIII's funeral carriage, designed by Lecointe and Hittorff, architects; body and axle system: Daldringen, the King's saddler/coachmaker; sculptures: Roguier; carvings, trim: Renault, master upholsterer.

Right-hand page:
Charles X's coronation carriage, built in 1821.

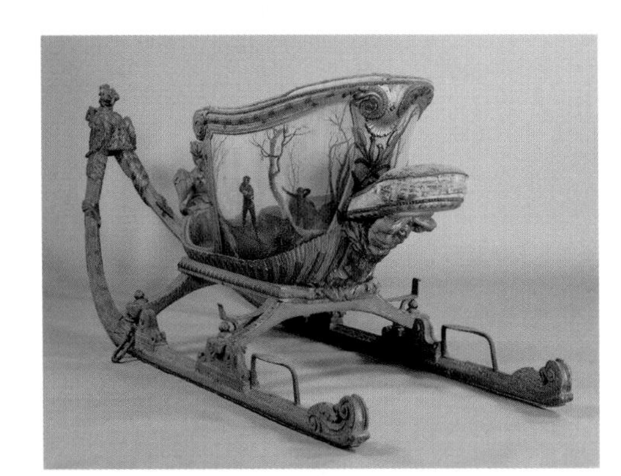

"Skater" sleigh, France, circa 1730, former royal collection.

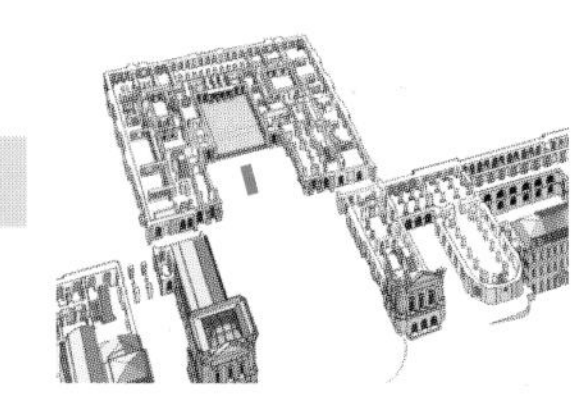

THE COURTYARDS AND FAÇADES

In front of the entry gate, a wide open space separates the stables from the château: this is the *Place d'Armes*, where the king inspected his army's regiments. Beyond the gate lie three courtyards, one after the other: the *Cour d'Honneur*, flanked by the Ministers' wings, followed by the Royal courtyard which was closed off under the *Ancien Régime* by a second gate, the restoration of which will soon be completed, and finally the Marble courtyard. It was through this second gate that access was gained to the actual "royal dwelling" and only the most esteemed personalities were permitted to pass through in their carriages. The Royal courtyard then entered is overlooked by buildings which differ from the others in terms of scale and the material used to construct them: stone. Work began on these buildings at the end of the reign of Louis XV. They were designed by the architect Gabriel who had the façades on the town side completely rebuilt in a classical style that was considered more noble at the time. The architecture of the façades, in brick and stone, topped by high slate roofs, actually dates back to the era of the first Château de Versailles built for Louis XIII, as Louis XIV retained it and had it extended in the same style. Although reworked, this original building still forms the heart of the château today.

The entrance gate, topped by the Coat of Arms of France.

At the end of the Marble Courtyard, the Lower Gallery and, above it, the balcony of the King's bedchamber.

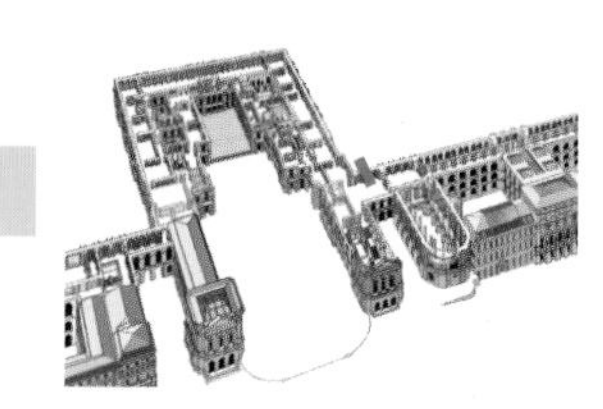

THE KING'S GRAND APARTMENT

FIRST FLOOR

The Grand Apartment consists of seven salons or drawing rooms overlooking the gardens on the north side through tall, floor-to-ceiling height windows, a novelty at the time of its creation in the 1670s. This prestigious sequence of rooms was designed to serve as a ceremonial apartment, in other words, as a backdrop for the official acts of the sovereign. It is for this reason that they were decorated with such sumptuousness and in the style of the Italian palaces of the era. The *Premier Peintre* (or Chief Painter to the King) Charles Le Brun, who was also the director of the Royal Academy of Painting and Sculpture and director of the Crown furniture manufactory, provided all the designs for the ceilings, the precious marble panelling, the furniture... right down to the door locks. But Louis XIV soon got into the habit of carrying out the core of his "royal duty" in his private apartment overlooking the Marble courtyard. So this Grand Apartment became a thoroughfare and a place for people to be received. During the day, it was open to everyone – French as well as foreign – who came to see the king there when he passed through on his way to the chapel or to admire the most splendid paintings in the royal collections. But three evenings per week, between All Saints Day and Easter, it was reserved for courtiers. From 7 o'clock to 10 o'clock, *"soirées d'appartement"* or court receptions were held consisting of music, dancing and games.

Above the fireplace:
Paul Veronese, *Eliezer and Rebecca*.

Next pages:
François Lemoine,
The Apotheosis of Hercules.

THE HERCULES SALON

The State Apartment's first salon, the Hercules Salon, was actually the last one to be created, at the end of the reign of Louis XIV. The location had previously been occupied by the château's chapel, created in 1682 on two floors and used until 1710, when it was replaced by the current chapel. To decorate this new salon, the monumental painting by Veronese, *Christ at Supper with Simon*, painted for the refectory of the Servite convent in Venice around 1570, was placed there in 1712. In 1664, the *Doge* had given the painting to Louis XIV to thank the latter for supporting him against the Turks. Interrupted for a period of ten years following the death of the Sun King, work on the Hercules Salon lasted until 1736, when François Lemoine completed the ceiling painting showing *The Apotheosis of Hercules*, designed to depict the fact that "Virtue elevates man above himself". Through its effect, this vast allegorical composition containing 142 figures was intended to rival the great masterpieces of the Italian fresco painters but it was actually done on canvases that were then mounted on the ceiling, i.e. that were stuck onto the medium. The process was so exhausting that, in spite of the success his work met with, the young painter committed suicide shortly afterwards.

THE KING'S GRAND APARTMENT

FIRST FLOOR

THE ABUNDANCE SALON

During *"soirées d'appartement"*, the Abundance Salon was where refreshments were taken; coffee, wines and liqueurs were available on a sideboard. It was also the antechamber of Louis XIV's Cabinet of Curiosities or Rarities (now occupied by Louis XVI's Games room) which could be reached through the door at the end. The King liked to show his distinguished guests the silver vases, gemstones and medals that were kept there and which inspired the décor of the arch. In particular, the large royal ship represented above the door can be admired.

The king's ship, a precious object in the form of a dismasted boat, was placed on the sovereign's table for grand occasions, or, of course, on the sideboard. A symbol of power to be saluted by every passer-by, it contained the sovereign's napkin.

The King's Ship.

Below:
René-Antoine Houasse, *Asian figure*.

THE VENUS SALON

Along with the Diana Salon, this salon represented the main access to the State Apartments since the state staircase, known as the "Ambassadors' Staircase" (destroyed in 1752) led to this room. On state evenings, tables were set out with baskets of flowers, pyramids of fresh and rare fruits such as oranges and lemons as well as crystallized fruit and marzipan. As is the case with each of the subsequent rooms, this salon is named after a planet, a theme linked to the solar myth that inspired all the décors at Versailles in the 1670s. Here the planet Venus is represented on the ceiling, in the form of the goddess of Love, who was linked with this planet in Ancient Greece. The other paintings, adorning the spring of the vault (ceiling panels), were designed to depict the actions of ancient heroes relating both to the planet of the same name and the actions of Louis XIV: hence the panel representing *Augustus presiding over circus games* should be seen as referring to the famous carousel of 1662 given in honour of the queen and the one depicting *Alexander marrying Roxane* as evoking the marriage of Louis XIV.

Of all the rooms in the sequence, the Venus Salon has the most baroque decor. It is the only room where Le Brun created a dialogue between the architectures, the sculptures and the paintings, sometimes real and sometimes false: the marble pilasters and columns are echoed in the perspectives painted by Jacques Rousseau, and two trompe l'œil statues on the window side are a repost to the figure of Louis XIV by Jean Warin.

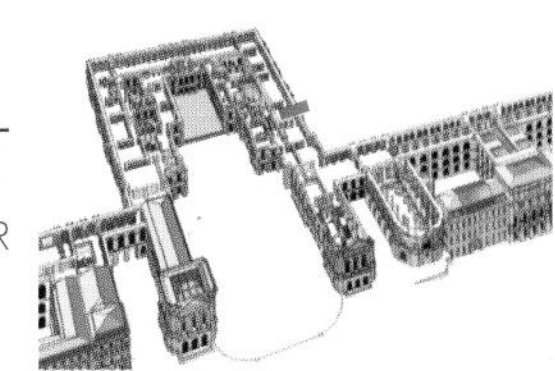

Bernini, *Bust of Louis XIV at twenty-seven years old.*

THE DIANA SALON

Like the Venus Salon, the Diana Salon served as a vestibule to the State Apartments and, during the time of Louis XIV, as a billiard room during *"soirées d'appartement"*. Two special platforms were reserved for the ladies who applauded whenever the king, who was very skilled at the game, hit a good shot. So much so that the room was also called "the room of applause". In Greek Antiquity, Diana the Goddess of Hunting was associated with the moon, for her coldness. She was also the sister of Apollo, the Sun God. The ceiling panels are adorned with hunting scenes involving heroes from Antiquity. Here, the allusion is transparent as it is well known that Louis XIV was a great huntsman.

The central part of the ceiling painted by Gabriel Blanchard depicts *Diana presiding over navigation and hunting*.
On the fireplace, the painting by Charles de La Fosse depicting *The Sacrifice of Iphigenia* and, opposite, above the console, *Diana and Endymion* by Gabriel Blanchard. The classical busts come from the collections of Cardinal de Mazarin bequeathed to Louis XIV.

THE KING'S GRAND APARTMENT
FIRST FLOOR

THE MARS SALON

As well as being a planet, Mars is also the God of War. The choice of this military theme that was to inspire the decoration throughout this large room can be explained by the fact that it was originally designed as the guardroom for the ceremonial apartment. It was subsequently used for music and dancing on state evenings and hence came to be commonly known as the "ballroom". Court dances were very formal and required numerous rehearsals; princes took part in them, sometimes alongside professional dancers. On either side of the fireplace, two platforms, removed in 1750, were intended for the musicians.

In the centre of the ceiling, Claude Audran painted Mars on a chariot drawn by wolves. The work is flanked by two compositions; one, on the east side, by Jouvenet: *Victory supported by Hercules followed by Abundance and Felicity*; the other, on the west side, by Houasse: *Terror, Fury and Fear taking possession of earthly powers*. Four paintings by Simon Vouet, originally in the château de Saint-Germain-en-Laye are placed above the doors: *Temperance*, *Prudence*, *Justice* and *Fortitude.*
David playing the harp by Dominichino, Louis XIV's favourite painting placed above the fireplace, used to be in the alcove of the King's bedchamber in Louis XIV's time and was a matching piece to a *Saint Jean in Patmos*, at the time attributed to Raphael.
To the left of the fireplace can be seen *The Family of Darius before Alexander*, by Charles Le Brun and on the right *The Pilgrims of Emmaus*, based on the Veronese painting (previously the original): placed together as matching pieces, they reflect a determination to show that French painters could now rival the very best Italian masters. On the side walls are two ceremonial portraits: Louis XV and Maria Leszczinska, both painted by Carle Van Loo.

THE MERCURY SALON

Originally, the Mercury Salon was the ceremonial bedchamber of the state apartment, hence the name "bedchamber", although the bed in question was taken away during the winter to make room for games tables. Until 1689, when Louis XIV was forced to melt them down in order to finance the war of the League of Augsburg, tables, mirrors, fire-dogs and chandeliers of solid silver magnificently chiselled by the silversmiths of the Les Gobelins manufactory adorned the walls, ceilings and fireplace. A balustrade, also made of silver, separated the alcove from the rest of the room. Brocades – fabrics woven using gold and silver threads – hung on the walls and the bed but these too were sent to the Mint, this time to support the Spanish War of Succession. One of the rare occasions on which the Mercury Salon was used as a bedroom was for the proclamation of the Duke of Anjou, the grandson of Louis XIV, as King of Spain: the young prince slept in it for three weeks, before going to his new country. It is also in this room that the body of Louis XIV was displayed from 2 to 10 September 1715.

The War of the League of Augsburg, also known as the "Nine years War" or the "War of the Grand Alliance" was triggered in 1688 by France's occupation of the Palatinate. In response to this action, the Empire, the Netherlands and Spain formed an alliance to contest the kingdom's claims concerning the right of *Madame* (the Duchess of Orleans), the sister-in-law of Louis XIV and Princess Palatine, to the territory. This conflict, the most important during Louis XIV's reign, ended with Strasbourg being ceded to France, on 30 October 1697. The Spanish War of Succession followed Louis XIV's acceptance of the testament of Charles II who, having died without an heir, appointed the Duke of Anjou as his successor at the head of all Spain's possessions and hence gave preference to the Bourbon dynasty over the Habsburg dynasty, from which he came.

Opposite: Louis Tocqué, *Maria Leszczinska*. facing a portrait of Louis XV by Hyacinthe Rigaud.

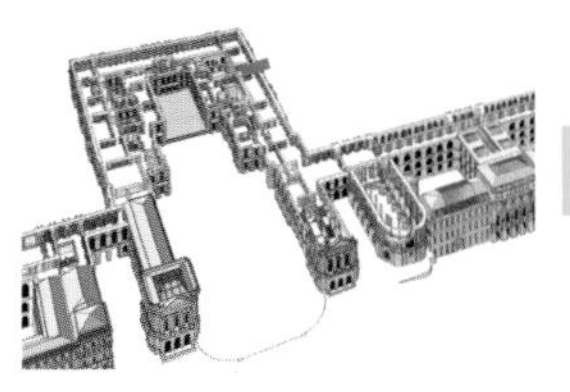

THE MERCURY SALON

Antoine Morand,
Automation clock.
Only the celebrated automation clock that its designer, Antoine Morand, gave to Louis XIV in 1706 has been able to be put back in the place it occupied up until the Revolution.

The ceiling painted by Jean-Baptiste de Champaigne depicts *Mercury on his chariot drawn by two cockerels*. The vaulted ceiling panels are decorated with four paintings: on the left, on the Mars Salon side, *Augustus receiving an Ambassador of the Indians*; at the end, opposite the windows, *Ptolemy consulting scholars in his library;* on the right, on the window side, *Alexander and Aristotle* receiving from this prince a variety of strange animals for which he writes their story. The bed that can be seen now is the one Louis-Philippe had installed in the King's Bedchamber when he converted Versailles into a museum.

THE KING'S GRAND APARTMENT

FIRST FLOOR

THE APOLLO SALON

The Apollo Salon, dedicated to the Sun God, God of the Arts and Peace with whom Louis XIV identified himself, was the most sumptuous of all. This can still be seen today in the décor of the ceiling where all the paintings – central composition, panels and corner pieces– are all in glorious colour and the sculptures are in the round and all gilded. But everything else has gone: the silver furniture, and in particular the 2.6 metre high throne, was melted down in 1689. A gilded wooden chair, the style of which evolved with the various reigns, replaced the throne of Louis XIV. It was placed on a platform covered with a Persian carpet with a gold background and under a canopy. The hangings which, as in all royal households, were changed according to the season, were in crimson velvet punctuated by eighteen strips of gold and silver embroidery in the winter, and silver and gold embroideries on a silk background in the summer.

Hyacinthe Rigaud, *Louis XIV* (Right-hand page). It is a matching piece for the portrait of Louis XVI, by Antoine-François Callet.

On the ceiling (see the next page), *Apollo on his chariot drawn by four horses and accompanied by the seasons* was painted by Charles de La Fosse.

> Comte d'Hézecques, *Recollections of a Page in Louis XVI's Court*
>
> *"In the first drawing room [...] named after Apollo, was a throne of crimson damask on a dais, but it was never used. The King very rarely held his audiences from atop the throne, at least not from that one. In the same room, a crystal thermometer was attached to the window, and the King would come and check the temperature several times a day. In addition, a footman would record the degrees in his register three times a day."*

THE SALON OF WAR

The Salon of War, the Hall of Mirrors and the Salon of Peace make up an ensemble that is almost 100 metres in length, finishing off the sequence of rooms in the State Apartments magnificently. It was not always like this as, until 1678, there were three additional rooms to the State Apartments which led to a terrace. At that point, the end of the Franco-Dutch War was an opportunity to consider new building work and a change. The architect Hardouin-Mansart built the Hall and the two salons. Le Brun designed the decoration before, between 1681 and 1684, producing the paintings with the help of his studio. The solar myth then gave way to the themes of war and peace and the king is no longer represented as Apollo but triumphant, dressed as a Roman Emperor.
The signing of the Treaty of Nijmegen in 1678 marked the height of the reign. The paintings adorning the Salon of War exalt the victories of France over the European powers united against her: the Empire, Spain and Holland.

Antoine Coysevox, *Chained prisoner*.

THE HALL OF MIRRORS

Following the victory over the three united powers represented in the Salon of War and mentioned on the previous page, the 73-metre long hall exalts France's political, economic and artistic success. Political success: the thirty compositions on the vaulted ceiling painted by Le Brun illustrate the glorious story of Louis XIV during the first eighteen years of his personal government, from 1661 until the Nijmegen Peace Treaty. Thus, military and diplomatic victories along with reforms to reorganise the kingdom are illustrated in the form of classical allegories. Economic prosperity: through their dimensions and number, the 357 mirrors adorning the seventeen arcades opposite the windows testify that the new French mirror industry is capable of taking away Venice's monopoly on mirrors, considered to be objects of immense luxury at the time. Artistic success: the Rance marble pilasters are adorned with a new design - the so-called "French order" - of gilded bronze capitals; created by Le Brun at the request of Colbert, it depicts the emblems of France: a fleur de lys surmounted by the royal sun between two French cockerels.

Léopold Delbeke,
The Hall of Mirrors prepared for signature of the Versailles Peace Treaty, on 28 June 1919.

THE HALL OF MIRRORS AND ITS SALONS

FIRST FLOOR

THE HALL OF MIRRORS

The *Grande Galerie* or Great Gallery as it was named in the 17th century, was a thoroughfare and meeting place frequented daily by courtiers and the visiting public. It was only rarely used for ceremonial purposes, when the sovereigns wanted to lend as much glamour as possible to diplomatic receptions or the entertainment (balls and games) provided for the marriages of princes. For the former, the throne was set up on a platform at the end of the hall, at the Salon of Peace end, the arcade to which was closed off. Only rarely did the display of power achieve such a degree of ostentation; hence the Doge of Genoa in 1685 and the ambassadors of Siam (1686), Persia (1715) and the Ottoman Empire (1742) had to cross the entire length of the hall, under the eyes of the Court assembled on either side on terraces! There were also the marriages of the Duke of Burgundy, the grandson of Louis XIV in 1697, the son of Louis XV in 1745 and finally the masked ball for the marriage of Marie-Antoinette and the Dauphin, the future Louis XVI, in May 1770... It is also here that on 28 June 1919 the Treaty of Versailles bringing an end of the First World War was signed. Since then, the Presidents of the Republic have continued to play host to the official guests of France in this hall.

Claude Hallé, *Audience granted by Louis XIV to the Doge of Genoa on 15 May 1685.* The detail on the right shows the silver furniture and, in particular, the throne.

Charles Le Brun, *The King governs by himself,* 1661, central ceiling composition.

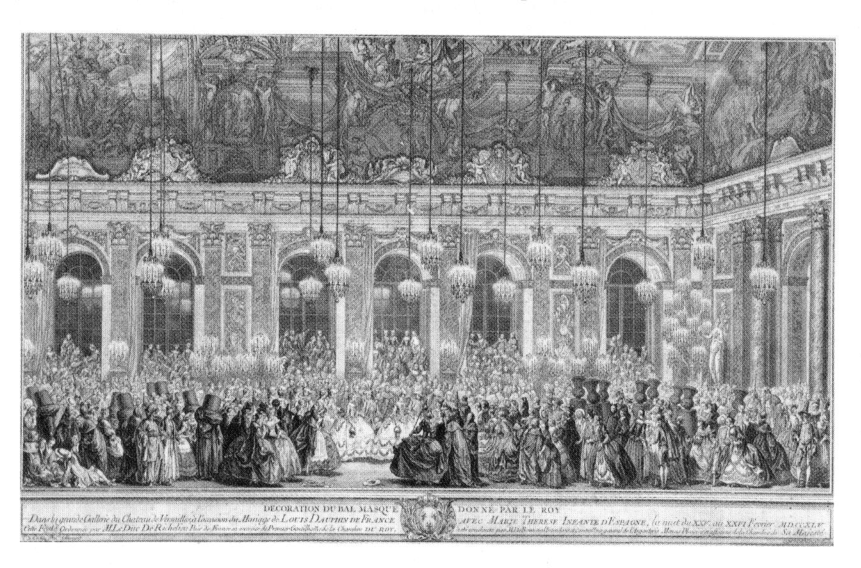

Charles Nicolas Cochin (the Younger), *Masked ball given for the marriage of Louis Dauphin of France to Maria Theresa of Spain in Versailles in February 1745; Hall of Mirrors (The Yew Tree Ball).*

THE SALON OF PEACE

The Salon of Peace presents the same décor of marble panels and gilded and chiselled bronze trophies of arms as the Salon of War, which is symmetrical to it. However, Le Brun adorned the dome and the ceiling panels with the benefits of peace given by France to Europe. From the end of the reign of Louis XIV, this salon was separated from the hall by a mobile partition and considered to be part of the Queen's Suite, forming, as it then did, its first room. It was here that, under the reign of Louis XV, Maria Leszczinska gave secular or religious music concerts every Sunday which were to play an important role in the musical life of Versailles. It was also here that Marie-Antoinette hosted her card games during the next reign.

The ceiling, which is the work of Le Brun, depicts *Victorious France offering an olive branch to the Powers that had united against her.* The vaulted ceiling panels depict *Spain, Christian Europe at peace, Germany* and *Holland.* Above the fireplace, the large oval canvas painted by François Lemoine in 1729 shows *Louis XV giving peace to Europe.* The gilded bronze "firedogs" in the form of lions, created on the basis of a model by Boizot, were put there by Marie-Antoinette.

THE QUEEN'S SUITE

FIRST FLOOR

Overlooking the *parterre du Midi* or South parterre, the Queen's Suite is symmetrical to the King's Grand Apartment. But, unlike the sovereign who, from the reign of Louis XIV, abandoned his State Apartments, the queen continued to occupy hers, which explains why the décor was altered several times during the course of the 18th century. Following the death of Queen Maria Theresa in 1683, it was occupied successively by two dauphines, Marie-Christine of Bavaria and Marie-Adelaide of Savoy, then by the two queens, Maria Leszczinska (from 1725 to 1768) and Marie-Antoinette (from 1770, when she was still dauphine, until 1789). It comprises four rooms which can be toured today, from the bedchamber to the guardroom, the exact opposite to the way it was used under the *Ancien Régime*.

Jean-Baptiste Gautier-Dagoty, *Marie-Antoinette placing the harp in her bedchamber in Versailles.*

The furniture in the bedchamber was restored during the 1980s; the bedchamber is now similar to how it would have been in Marie-Antoinette's time.

THE QUEEN'S BEDCHAMBER

The bedchamber is the suite's principal room, where the queen would most often be found. She slept there, often joined by the king. In the mornings she received both during and after her *toilette,* a time in the court timetable that was as regulated as when the king rose from his bed. It was also here that royal births took place in public: nineteen "Children of France" were born there. The décor preserves the memory of the three queens who occupied the room: the partitioning of the ceiling dates back to Queen Maria Theresa, but the paintings in grisaille by Boucher were done for Maria Leszczinska, as was the panelling. All these features have been preserved since the time of Marie-Antoinette, for whom only the furniture and fireplace were delivered new.

THE QUEEN'S SUITE

FIRST FLOOR

THE QUEEN'S BEDCHAMBER

When the château was invaded by the mob on 6 October 1789, Marie-Antoinette managed to escape through one of the two small alcove doors which give access to the queen's private rooms, of which there were a dozen reserved for her private life and her servants. When the Revolution took place, the château was not plundered, but the furniture was sold off at auctions which lasted an entire year. Some items were rediscovered, such as the Schwerdfeger jewel-casket to the left of the bed or the fire-screen, whilst others were replaced with equivalent items: such as, for example, the seats delivered for the Countess of Provence, the queen's sister-in-law for the visit of King Gustav III of Sweden. As for the fabrics hanging around the bed and on the walls, they were re-woven in Lyons in the style of the original cartoons that had been kept. The bed and balustrade were recarved based on old documents.

On the walls are hung the "summer coverings" that were in place on the night of 6 October 1789, when the royal family and the court left Versailles for the last time.

Louis XVI, old reproduction by Joseph-Siffrein Duplessis.

Michel-Henri Cozette, *Maria Theresa of Austria*, mother of Marie-Antoinette, Gobelins tapestry from a portrait by Joseph Ducreux.

Michel-Henri Cozette, *Joseph II*, brother of Marie-Antoinette, Gobelins tapestry from a portrait by Joseph Ducreux.

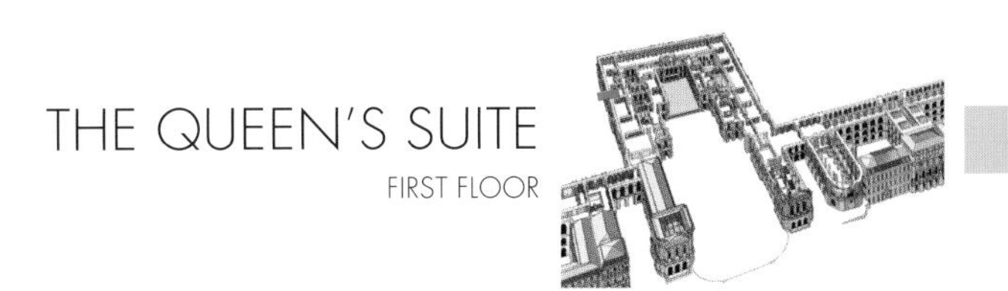

THE PEERS' SALON

The antechamber under Queen Maria Theresa, it is in this room that Maria Leszczinska granted her formal audiences, sitting under a canopy. It was also there that she held her *cercle* or circle, as this formal conversation with the ladies of the Court was known. Marie-Antoinette had the decoration completely changed, only retaining the ceiling paintings and for her, the walls were adorned with apple-green damask trimmed with wide gold braid. New furniture was delivered which was both modern and refined. For the majestic commodes and corner pieces designed for this room, Riesener, the queen's favourite cabinet-maker, conformed to the latest English fashion, abandoning his habitual floral marquetry for large mahogany inlays while the gilded bronzes as well as the turquin blue plates of this majestic ensemble were matched with those of the fireplace, it too new.

The portrait of Louis XV in royal costume, executed in tapestry by Cozette from a painting by L.-M. Van Loo was already in the same place in Marie-Antoinette's time.

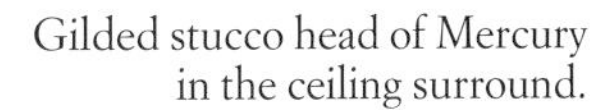

Gilded stucco head of Mercury in the ceiling surround.

Relief frieze on the arching: winged cherubs holding *Account Ledgers*.

THE ANTECHAMBER FOR *GRAND COUVERT* REPASTS

It is in the queen's antechamber that public meals were taken, a lavish ritual which attracted quite a crowd. Only the royal family were allowed to take their seats at table. In front of them were the duchesses, princesses or high office-bearers who were privileged enough to sit on stools. There were then the other ladies and people who, by rank or with the permission of ushers, had been allowed to enter. They had to stand. Louis XIV forced himself to attend this event almost every evening; for his part, Louis XV preferred a more intimate dinner with friends; as for Louis XVI and Marie-Antoinette, accounts from the period report that "The Queen sat to the left of the King. They had their backs to the fireplace [...] The King ate heartily, but the Queen did not remove her gloves and did not use her napkin, which is very poor manners." To counter her boredom, Marie-Antoinette requested that there should always be music in the *Grand Couvert* and for this purpose a platform was installed in the room for the musicians.

Adélaïde Labille-Guiard,
Madame Elisabeth,
Louis XVI's aunt.

Right-hand page:
Élisabeth Vigée-Lebrun,
Marie-Antoinette and her children
(Madame Royale, the first dauphin, who died in 1789, and the Duke of Normandy, future Louis XVII).

THE QUEEN'S SUITE

FIRST FLOOR

THE QUEEN'S GUARDS ROOM

The Queen's staircase, also known as the Marble staircase, gave access to the Queen's Suite through this Guardroom in which, night and day, twelve body guards served the queen. At Versailles, only the king, the queen and the dauphin were able to have a personal guard made up of soldiers belonging to these elite units which were the king's four companies of body guards. The next large room, known today as the "Coronation room", was allocated to them and served as the guardroom.

The Queen's Guard Room is the only room in the suite to have retained the 17th century décor: as the queen never had occasion to be there, it was never deemed necessary to modernise it. It is for this reason that the marble wall panels characteristic of the original State Apartments along with the paintings placed there in 1680, from the Jupiter Salon, which became the Salon of War, can still be seen.

Orders for the Queen's Sentinel

The sentinel of the Queen's room will not allow any unknown priests or friars to pass without the Captain's permission; even with the Captain's permission, he will not allow them to enter the Grand Couvert unless under special orders.

He will not allow any unknown person, anyone who looks unwell or any person recently afflicted by smallpox to pass.

No sedan chairs other than those of the Royal Family, or princes and princesses of royal blood are to remain in the room.

The presence of liverymen is not permitted.

The livery of the princes and princesses of royal blood, the Chevalier of the Legion of Honour, ladies-in-waiting and mistresses of the robes, and the chief chaplain to the Queen will go through into the antechamber.

He will allow only one servant of the cardinals and ministers to pass.

CONSIGNE

DE LA SENTINELLE DE LA REINE

Il ne laissera passer aucune autre personne inconnue, de mauvaise mine ou nouvellement marquée de la Petite Vérolle.

Il ne restera dans la salle d'autres chaises à porteurs, que celles de la Famille Royalle, des Princes et Princesses du sang.

Il n'y souffrira rester aucun homme de livrée.

Il laissera passer un seul domestique des Cardinaux et des Ministres,

Noël Coypel, *Sacrifice to Jupiter.*

Comte d'Hézecques, *Recollections of a Page in Louis XVI's Court*

"In the château, the bodyguards' duty was to stand guard at the doors of the apartments, man their weapons when the princes passed, fill up the chapel during Mass and escort the Royal Family to dinner. They had to be able to recognise dukes and other peers, because the sentinel had to present arms and click his right heel twice when these persons passed. In addition, this sentinel had to open the door and keep it from being opened; but this guard seemed to be rather easy going, and was excluded from all of these functions."

THE CORONATION ROOM

FIRST FLOOR

This large room was completely transformed in the 19th century when King Louis-Philippe turned Versailles into a museum recounting the history of France up to his own reign through paintings and sculptures. It is therefore attached to the history galleries which today occupy a significant part of the château's wings and other spaces. The paintings there refer to the Napoleonic era, and its name stems from the presence of David's famous composition depicting the crowning ceremony – and not strictly speaking a coronation – of Napoleon I and Josephine, which took place in Notre-Dame de Paris cathedral, on 2 December 1804.
Under the *Ancien Régime*, it was the large guardroom which, due to its dimensions and neutral décor, was used for a variety of occasions: for the washing of the feet ceremonies on Maundy Thursday, for "beds of justice" through which the king imposed his will on Parliament and even marriage feasts...

Two major works: one by David, *The Distribution of Eagles at the Champ de Mars* (1804),and the other by Gros, *The Battle of Aboukir* (1799), cover the east and north walls. The over-door panels painted by Gérard depict *Courage*, *Genius*, *Generosity* and *Constance*.
On the ceiling, the *Allegory of 18 Brumaire* is a work by Callet.
The bronze and porcelain column in the centre of the room, commissioned by Napoleon I commemorates the Battle of Austerlitz (2 December 1805).

Right-hand page:
Jacques-Louis David,
The Coronation of Napoleon I and Josephine, on 2 December 1804 (detail), replica painted by David himself, between 1808 and 1822 from the first version, today displayed in the Louvre.

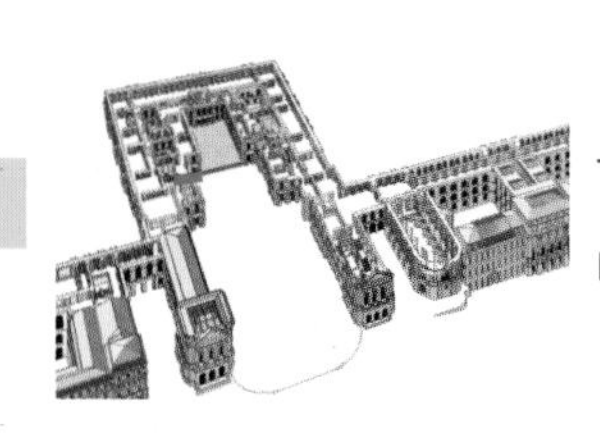

THE KING'S SUITE

FIRST FLOOR

Traditionally, the king had two apartments: a ceremonial apartment for official events and a private apartment for his personal life, but soon after the definitive installation of the Court at Versailles in 1682 and the death of Queen Maria Theresa the following year, Louis XIV had a suite of rooms designed around the Marble Courtyard which became his principal living quarters. He held both public and private events here, giving the latter a new official character. This life, which was one of perpetual performance and one in which every moment was governed by etiquette, was imposed upon his successors, who nevertheless had areas designed that they could retreat to. But until the end of the *Ancien Régime*, the King's Suite remained the power base of the crown. In its current state, the King's Suite comprises five rooms: a guardroom, two antechambers, the bedchamber and the council cabinet.

Charles Le Brun (attributed to), *The young Louis XIV.*

THE MARBLE STAIRCASE

This staircase, also known as the Queen's staircase, was the most used by the Court as it led both to the King's Suite and the Queen's Suite and, under Louis XIV, the apartment of Madame de Maintenon, whom the King married secretly upon the death of Maria Theresa. It was built in 1681, to match the Ambassadors' Staircase located at the other side of the courtyard. The richness of the décor stems above all from its ornamental paving and panelling composed of a variety of types of marble. It was Colbert who had ordered the kingdom's quarries to be prospected and developed and the marble that came from them is remarkable both in terms of the quality of the raw material and the way it has been worked.

THE ŒIL-DE-BŒUF SALON

This second antechamber, where courtiers waited to be admitted to the King's bedchamber, owes its name, literally "the bulls eye salon", to the oval window located in the ceiling frieze. Its dimensions and décor are the results of the renovations ordered by Louis XIV in 1701 to replace two approximately equally-sized rooms that had previously been there for seventeen years: one was a small antechamber and the other the King's bedchamber. The latter having become too small due to the number of courtiers present at his ceremonial rising in the morning, Louis XIV had it moved to its current location. The new, much bigger antechamber was decorated in a new style since Louis XIV, weary of splendour, wanted "youthfulness strewn everywhere". The ring of children adorning the frieze meets this requirement and its charm heralded the art of the 18th century.

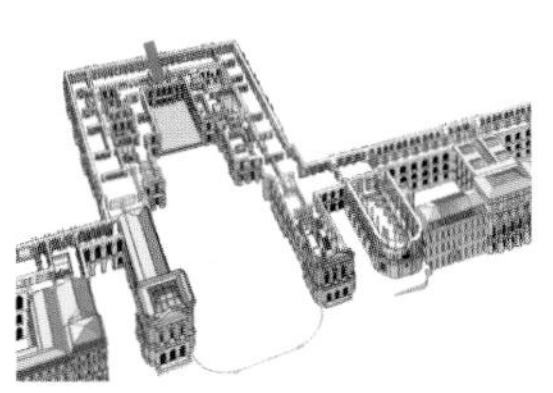

François Marot, *Inauguration of the Knights of the Order of Saint-Louis,* held in the King's bedchamber.

Valck Gerrit, *A Swiss Guard of the king.*

THE KING'S BEDCHAMBER

It was in 1701 that the King's Bedchamber, the genuine heart of Court life, came to be located in the centre of the château. When the king was there, access to it was strictly governed by etiquette, but in his absence, anyone could visit it, which astonished contemporaries. Louis XIV slept there, but his successors had another smaller bedchamber installed that was more comfortable. They did, however, continue to observe the ceremonial *"Lever"* (rising) and *"Coucher"* (retiring) rituals. The rising ritual lasted almost an hour, consisting of six successive entrances which marked the rank of each courtier. The *"Petit Lever"* took place when the King rose from his bed at around 8.30 in the morning, to be washed, shaved and have his hair attended to; for the small number of people admitted it was an opportunity to speak with the king and court favours. Then, during the *"Grand Lever"*, the king was dressed in front of several hundred people. Louis XIV returned to his bedchamber at around 1 o'clock in the afternoon to dine *"au petit couvert"* (lesser service), in other words alone at table, but always in the presence of the men of the Court. The bedchamber was also where individual audiences were held – or ceremonial audiences for ambassadors – and swearing-in ceremonies for the highest offices. It is the only space in the château that was not transformed by his successors who kept the masterpieces of the royal collections embedded in the panelling.

Next pages: The room retained its original décor after the Revolution and, in particular, some of its paintings: *The Four Evangelists* and *Caesar's Denarius* by Valentin de Boulogne, Saint John the Baptist by Carraciolo, *Mary Magdalene* by Dominichino, *Self Portrait and Portrait of the Marquis de Moncade* by Van Dyck.

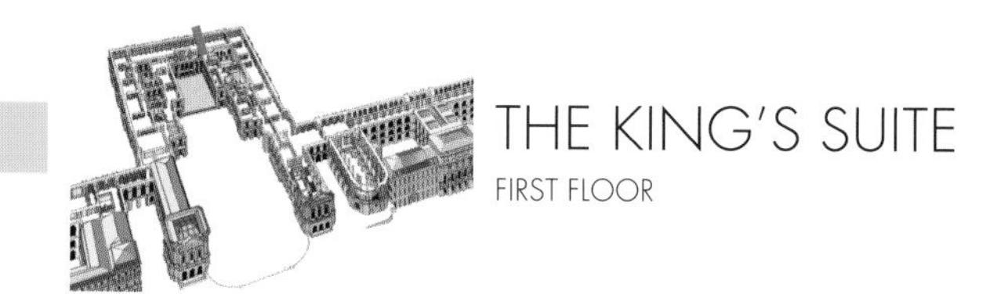

THE COUNCIL CABINET

Louis XIV had two rooms here; in one, the King held council daily from 11 o'clock in the morning to 1 o'clock in the afternoon: "On Sunday, and often on Monday, there was a Council of State; on Tuesday a Finance Council; on Wednesday Council of State; on Saturday finance council [...] Thursday morning was almost always blank. It was also the grand day taken advantage of by the bastard, *the Batîments*, the valets, etc., because the King had nothing to do. On Friday after the mass the King was with his confessor, and the length of their audiences was limited by nothing, and might last until dinner." (Saint-Simon, *Memoirs*).
In 1755, Louis XV turned it into a single room in which the panelling, designed by Gabriel and carved by Antoine Rousseau, depicts the various government departments such as the marine department and the war department... For more than a century, all major political decisions were taken in this room, including, in 1775, France's involvement in the American War of Independence.

Detail of the woodwork.

Detail of the fireplace.

THE KING'S PRIVATE APARTMENTS

FIRST FLOOR

The King's Private Apartments and the neighbouring cabinets look out onto the Marble courtyard and the Royal courtyard on the right. Laid out under the reign of Louis XV, they begin with a small guardroom on the ground floor to protect access to the king's staircase. This leads to the first floor and two antechambers (the *anti-chambre* des chiens or dogs' antechamber and the dining room for returning hunting parties), a bedchamber and a large cabinet preceding a suite of rooms for specific uses. It was there that royal collections had been displayed under Louis XIV: painting cabinet, book cabinet, shell cabinet as well as the small gallery decorated by Mignard, Le Brun's rival, in which the famous *Mona Lisa* by Leonardo da Vinci was kept.

LOUIS XV'S BEDCHAMBER

Not far from the large Louis XIV's bedchamber which was as impractical as it was majestic, Louis XV had a new bedchamber designed in 1738 that was smaller and south-facing, hence easier to heat. The sculptor Jacques Verbeckt designed the panelling and in particular the large palm trees and royal arms which decorate the alcove partition. The only modifications ordered for Louis XVI involved creating an invaluable little dressing room reached through a small door on the left and commissioning the delivery of new furniture, including the gold-embroidered half-damask reproducing the alcove hanging that was there in 1789.

THE CLOCK CABINET

Louis XV took a keen interest in sciences and, in particular, astronomy. Seen here on the floor of this cabinet is the Paris meridian embodied by a copper strip. The extraordinary clock, which gave the room its name, was presented to the Academy of Sciences and then to the King in Choisy before being moved here in 1754.

The clock indicates the time, the day of the week, the month, the year and the phases of the moon; in the crystal sphere, the planets can be seen revolving around the sun. The clock designed by Passemant, the King's engineer, executed by the clockmaker Dauthiau and the bronze case of which was made by Caffiéri, is an artistic and scientific monument. The crystal sphere at the top contains the sun and the planets, moving according to Copernicus' system. In addition to the time, it also indicates the year, the day of the week, the month and its date, along with the phase of the moon. It was used to set an official time throughout the kingdom for the very first time.

THE KING'S INNER CABINET

This "corner cabinet", as it was commonly known, looks out onto both the Marble courtyard and the royal courtyard. Louis XV was often there and it is from the balcony that he watched, his eyes filled with tears, the departure of Madame de Pompadour's funeral procession, one winter's evening in 1764. Although it was redecorated several times during his reign, the décor of the panelling remains one of the most beautiful works of Jacques Verbeckt who carved the panels in 1753. This room had the furniture made for it, in particular the roll-top "secretary" or desk ordered from Œben in 1760 and finished by Riesener nine years later. It was the first piece of furniture of this type and was a solution to the king's wishes to be able to leave his papers on his desk but sheltered from prying eyes. Remarkable for the beauty of its marquetry inlays and bronzes, it is also a mechanical marvel: a single quarter turn of the key simultaneously unlocked and locked the roll-top and all the drawers.

THE BATHROOM

The king's baths were amongst the last items commissioned by Louis XV. The style of the panelling, reproducing engravings evoking aquatic pleasures in medallions edged with reeds and narcissi, with matt gold, burnished gold and green gold effects, testify to a new taste. It was not Verbeckt, but his rival Antoine Rousseau, assisted by his son, who sculpted them in 1771. The bath was removed when Louis XVI installed his *pièce de la cassette* (or privy purse room) in which he kept records of his private accounts.

LOUIS XVI'S LIBRARY

This library, designed by the architect Gabriel shortly before the death of Louis XV in 1774, was one of Louis XVI's favourite rooms in which he indulged his passion for sciences and, particularly, geography. A globe of the earth carried by Atlas can be seen here, used by the king to trace the progress of great maritime adventures, especially that of La Pérouse which he had inspired and supported, as well as the large Riesener table, the top of which is made from a single piece of mahogany, 2.10 metres in diameter, and which is raised on jacks as Louis XVI needed a perfectly flat surface to mark out his corrections to geographic maps.

THE PORCELAIN DINING ROOM

This dining room, created for Louis XV in 1769 for his post-hunt suppers, was used mainly by Louis XVI and Marie-Antoinette. Over a twenty-year period, around forty guests regularly sat around the extendable table for these so-called "society" meals, a new type of meal midway between the great official banquets and "private" meals. If the number of guests exceeded the number of seated places, the men had their buffet from the billiard table in the neighbouring room. This dining room is also called the Porcelain Salon as every year at Christmas, Louis XVI had the latest items from the Sèvres manufactory displayed there.

Small quarry for young dogs, *"Forhu at the end of the hunt"*, one of the Sèvres porcelain plaques produced at the request of Louis XVI and based on the *Louis XV Hunt*, tapestries by Jean-Baptiste Oudry.

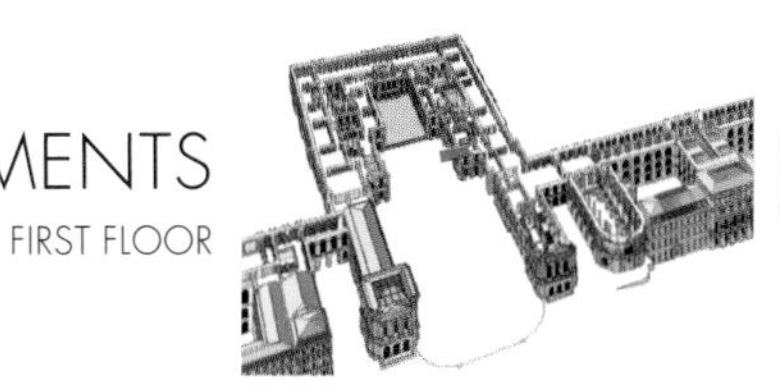

LOUIS XVI'S GAMES ROOM

Originally, Louis XIV's Cabinet of Curiosities was here, an extraordinary room of which there is no longer any trace. Having gone through various transitions, it is currently presented as it was at the time of Louis XVI when it was used as a games room. After a meal, guests withdrew there to take coffee. Louis XVI sat at a backgammon table whilst one of his brothers played billiards in the neighbouring room, the other whist. The furniture, sold in the Revolution, has largely been bought back: the four corner pieces ordered from Riesener in 1774 as well as the chairs delivered by Boulard in 1785. The works chosen by Louis XVI have also been put back on the walls: gouaches commemorating the military victories of his grandfather Louis XV, painted by Van Blarenberghe.

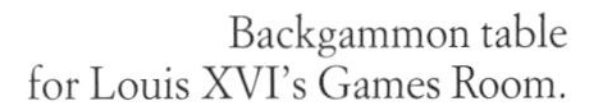

Backgammon table
for Louis XVI's Games Room.

THE KING'S SMALL CABINETS

FIRST FLOOR

A year after the Court returned to Versailles in 1722, stags' heads were placed on the façades of the king's courtyard. These were made of plaster and painted to make them more colourful in the eyes of the young Louis XV, then aged thirteen. Around this courtyard, now named the *Cour des Cerfs* or Stags' Courtyard, a maze of rooms was developed reserved for the sovereign's use, "charming little spaces that only his confidants had access to": the king's private cabinets. The layout, use and décor of these "rats' nests" were constantly altered at no small cost according to royal whims and, under Louis XV, included a library, a cabinet for turning ivory, kitchens, distilleries, jam-making rooms, a bathroom and, on an upper terrace, aviaries, as well as reception rooms for those who were lucky enough to be granted the much coveted favour of attending post-hunt suppers. Louis XV lived there, following the death of his wife, his last mistress, Madame Du Barry. Louis XVI had a carpentry room there, a wood-turning room, an ironworks, a room for mechanics, an electricity gallery...

The King's Staircase leading to the King's private cabinets.

Right-hand page:
Sequence of rooms in Madame Du Barry's apartment.

MARIE-ANTOINETTE'S PRIVATE CABINETS

FIRST FLOOR

On the other side of her Queen's Suite, the queen had some small rooms reserved for her own private use and that of her chambermaids. During the time of Louis XIV, Queen Maria Theresa only had an oratory and a boudoir there. Later, the queen had many more private rooms. Maria Leszczinska annexed the rooms from the main body of the building which separates the Queen's Courtyard from the Dauphin's Courtyard; she used to retire there to read, paint, meditate or receive her closest friends. Marie-Antoinette added further mezzanines and floors, to such an extent that she ended up with an entire private apartment on the ground floor looking out over the Marble Courtyard.
Generally speaking, the private areas – which were bare of any official character and therefore escaped the etiquette that dictated the exact nature of the furnishings,– mirrored changes in fashion to a greater extent that the State Apartments did. This was true for both the king and the queen. However, whilst Louis XVI was often quite happy with what had been done for his grandfather Louis XV, Marie-Antoinette was forever ordering new décors and new pieces of furniture.

THE GILDED STUDY

When she was at Versailles, it was to her inner cabinet– the biggest of the queen's private rooms – that Marie-Antoinette often retired to receive her children and friends, to play music with Grétry as her teacher, or pose for Madame Vigée-Lebrun, her favourite painter. Created for Maria Leszczinska, this room was redecorated in 1783 from designs by Richard Mique, Marie-Antoinette's architect. The panelling by the Rousseau brothers, adorned with classical sphinxes and tripods, alludes to the recent discovery of Pompeii and Herculaneum. The majority of the items of furniture and objets d'art seen there today belonged to the sovereign: for example, the commode, one of Riesener's most beautiful creations, delivered for her bedchamber in Marly, and the "Chinese" Sèvres vases on top of it, which come from her apartment in Saint-Cloud.
Through a small door to the left of the fireplace, this *Cabinet doré* or Gilded Study – so-called due to the profusion of gold on the panelling, the bronzes, the seats – opens into a small room painted in "vernis Martin" dating from the 1750s. It is the only original example of the vogue for this process that was an imitation of Chinese lacquer. The panelling there come from an inner cabinet of the apartment of Marie-Josèphe of Saxony located on the ground floor; it was Marie-Antoinette herself who had this décor created for her mother-in-law brought up to her own private rooms.

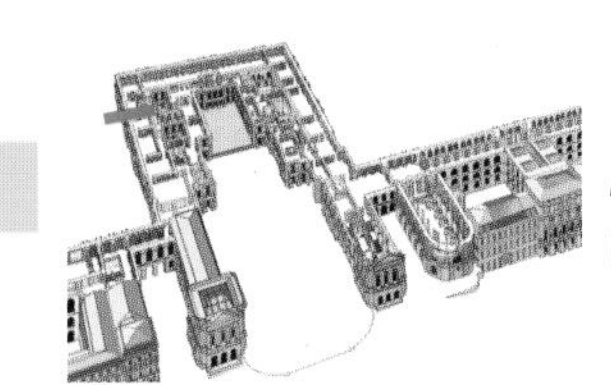

MARIE-ANTOINETTE'S PRIVATE CABINETS

FIRST FLOOR

THE MERIDIAN CABINET

The unusual shape of this boudoir, with its cut-off corners, enabled the queen's servants to move from the main bedchamber to the other rooms without disturbing the queen who, midway through the day, would come to rest there, hence the name Meridian. It was in 1781, once Marie-Antoinette had finally given birth to an heir, that the room was given its décor of panelling, the motifs of which can also be seen in bronze appliqués on the glazed doors. The dolphin seen there evokes the child, whilst the roses, the Habsburg eagle and the peacock, associated with the goddess Juno, are allusions to the queen herself.

THE BILLIARD CABINET

The queen had a few new private rooms fitted out on the second floor, in particular a dining room and a billiard room. The latter was decorated with silks and items of precious furniture: sofas by G. Jacob, jewellery box by Carlin.

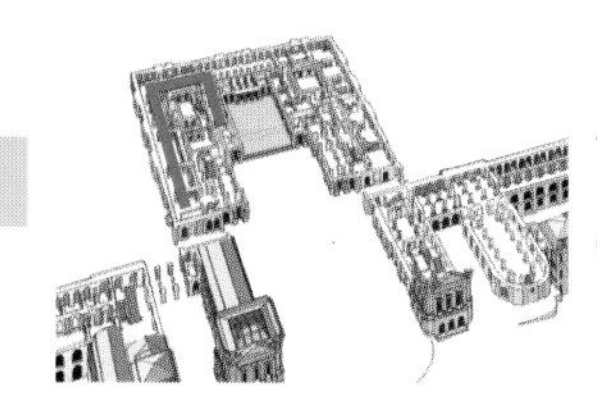

THE APARTMENTS OF THE DAUPHIN AND DAUPHINE

GROUND FLOOR

These ground floor apartments – which communicated directly with those of the queen located just above via several staircases – were always reserved for the leading members of the royal family. Notably, Louis XIV's brother, known as *Monsieur*, then his son known as *Monseigneur* were accommodated there. Finally his nephew, know as the Regent, who governed after his death, lived there. Their current state corresponds to the period when they were inhabited by Louis XV's son (Louis, dauphin of France) and by his second wife Marie-Josèphe of Saxony, that is to say between 1747 and 1765. For a long time occupied by the Count and Countess of Provence, the brother and sister-in-law of Louis XVI, they sheltered the young dauphin, the future Louis XVII, and his sister *Madame Royale* when the Revolution broke out.

The two apartments of the Dauphin and Dauphine are connected by their last room, which is also the most intimate one: the prince's library and the princess' inner cabinet, painted in "vernis Martin". Very close, the dauphin Louis and his wife Marie-Josèphe of Saxony went their often, leaving the connecting door open.

The Dauphin's library.

Right-hand page:
the Dauphine's inner cabinet.

THE APARTMENTS OF THE DAUPHIN AND DAUPHINE

GROUND FLOOR

THE DAUPHIN'S BEDCHAMBER

From the Marble courtyard, one goes through a Guardroom and two antechambers to reach the Dauphin's Bedchamber. The function of the room, as well as its dimensions and décor, date back to 1747. Before that time there had been a smaller room in its place, first the *Cabinet doré* (Gilded study) of *Monseigneur* who displayed his collection of paintings there, followed by the Regent's study. He was to die there in 1723. As for all the decoration work carried out during the time that he was the king's First architect (from 1742 to 1775), Gabriel supplied the designs for this bedchamber. As was the custom, silks were hung in the alcove whilst the rest of the room was panelled with carved oak (made in Jacques Verbeckt's workshop – it was he who produced most of the panelling destined for Versailles) highlighted in white and gold, in other words a white background with gilded motifs.

The Dauphine's bed having disappeared, it was replaced by a "duchess" bed – i.e. one in which the canopy is not held up by pillars – produced in around 1740 for the Marchioness de Créquy; its fabrics (opposite) are decorated with motifs of foliage and medallions produced in petit point needlework; the needlework on the headboard depicts the sleep of the shepherd Endymion.
To the right of the bed, the painting depicting a farm (above) is a copy produced by Queen Maria Leszczinska, from an original by Oudry kept in the Louvre; Jean-Baptiste Oudry was the queen's drawing teacher.

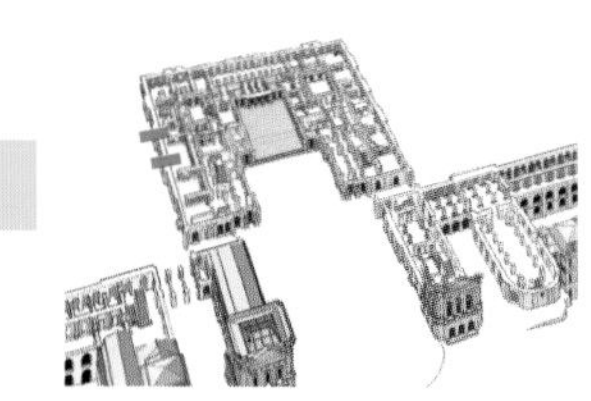

THE APARTMENTS OF THE DAUPHIN AND DAUPHINE

GROUND FLOOR

THE DAUPHINE'S BEDCHAMBER

It was in this bedchamber that the dauphine Marie-Josèphe of Saxony, daughter of King Augustus III of Poland and wife of Louis XV, gave birth to three future kings of France: Louis XVI, Louis XVIII and Charles X. Nothing remains of the décor it was given in 1747, with the exception of the panels over the doors painted by Jean Restout. The original bed was replaced with a beautiful "Polish-style" bed (with a dome-shaped canopy supported by four pillars) designed by Nicolas Heurtaut. On either side of the bed are portrayed the Dauphine's sisters-in-law, Louis XV's daughters, and in particular *Henriette of France as Flora* and *Marie-Adelaide of France as Diana*, painted by Jean-Marc Nattier.

Jean-Marc Nattier, *The Dauphine Marie-Josèphe of Saxony.*

THE DAUPHINE'S STATE CABINET

After the Dauphin's apartments, those of the Dauphine are visited in reverse order to the norm in terms of the succession of rooms, in other words: first and second antechambers, state cabinet, bedchamber and finally the private cabinet. In the state cabinet, the dimensions of which date back to the time when the room served as a guardroom for the guards of Louis XIV's son, Marie-Josèphe of Saxony assembled the ladies in her entourage for conversation or games. As was the case throughout the apartments, a new décor had been designed for her, but it disappeared in the 19th century on the orders of Louis-Philippe. Only the large console was spared and replaced under a mirror, the frame of which has been restored; it now supports a barometer produced for the future Louis XVI who, until his accession in 1774, occupied these apartments. On the "fire-coloured" wall covering, a modern version of the one described in inventories, were hung portraits of ministers and members of the Royal family from the beginning of the reign of Louis XV.

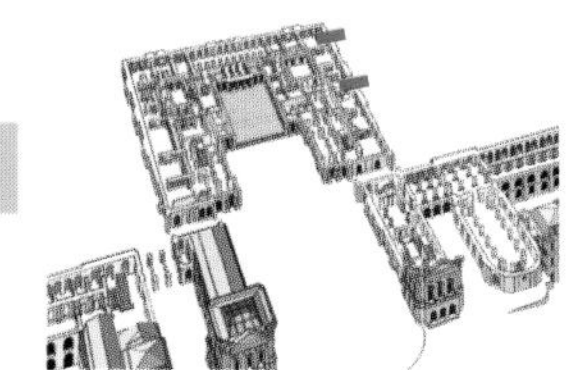

THE APARTMENTS OF MADAME VICTOIRE AND MADAME ADELAIDE

GROUND FLOOR

Beyond the Lower Gallery, the ladies' apartments are symmetrical to the apartments of the Dauphin and the Dauphine. Like these, they were transformed into a museum room by Louis-Philippe and have been recently restored as princes' apartments. *"Mesdames"*, as the six daughters of Louis XV were called, moved into these apartments in 1752, but only two of them, Adélaïde and Victoire – who did not marry, did not die and did not enter a convent – inhabited them until the Revolution.

MADAME VICTOIRE'S STATE CABINET

Originally, this was the octagonal cabinet of Louis XIV's Bathroom apartment, one of the most original creations of the Sun King, in which the opulence of the marbles, sculpture and paintings surpassed that of the State Apartment. In 1763, *Mesdames* were given permission to have the outdated décor changed; from this renovation remains the cornice, the panelling in the corners of the room as well as the beautiful fireplace. A Blanchet harpsichord is a reminder that Madame Victoire played this instrument admirably and that Mozart dedicated his first six harpsichord sonatas to her.

Jean-Marc Nattier's studio, *Madame Adelaide of France (1732-1799) reading the music from a violin score.*

MADAME ADELAIDE'S PRIVATE CABINET

This room was famous in its time as Madame de Pompadour's red lacquer cabinet. Indeed Louis XV's mistress, once she had become the king's "friend" in 1750, occupied what was later to become Madame Adelaide's apartment; moreover she died there in 1764. With its highly refined furniture and its souvenirs of the Château de Bellevue, the *Mesdames'* favourite residence, the current layout of Madame Adelaide's private cabinet is evocative of this princess who, according to the Countess of Boigne "had an extreme need for quests invented by luxury".

Jean-Baptiste Charpentier, *The Family of the Duke of Penthievre*, known as *The Cup of Chocolate*, 1768. his painting depicts a intimate scene from princely family life at the end of the reign of Louis XV: the Countess of Toulouse, the wife of a legitimate son of Louis XIV, is shown on the left, with her son the Duke of Penthievre (on the right) and her grandchildren, the Prince and Princess of Lamballe and the future Duchess of Orleans.

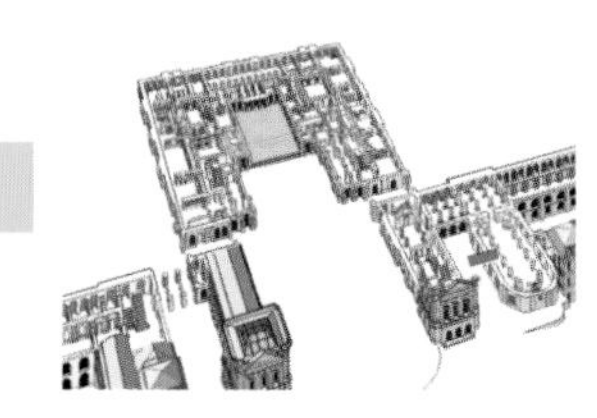

THE CHAPEL ROYAL

GROUND FLOOR

Louis XIV only used this chapel for five years since it was not finished until 1710. The one he used the most, built in 1682 where the Hercules Salon is now located, soon proved to be too cramped. However wars delayed work on the large chapel, begun in 1689 by Hardouin-Mansart. The architect never saw the building completed as he died in 1708. After his death, his brother-in-law, Robert de Cotte, took over, but the general lines of the architecture and the décor had been fixed in 1699: a design including a nave, aisles and ambulatory, an elevation with tribunes (or vaulted galleries), a harmony of white and gold contrasting with the polychrome of the ornamental marble tiling and vault paintings; the project resulted in an original work harking back to a blend of gothic architecture and baroque aesthetics.
Every day, usually at 10 a.m., the Court attended the King's Mass. The King himself would be in the royal tribune, surrounded by his family. The ladies of the Court occupied the side galleries. In the nave were the "officers" and the public. The king only went down there for major religious celebrations, for ceremonies of the order of the Holy Spirit, for baptisms and marriages of the Children of France celebrated there from 1710 to 1789.
Above the altar, around Cliquot's organ played by some grand masters such François Couperin, the *Musique de la Chapelle* (Chapel music choir), famous across Europe, sang anthems throughout the daily services.

In the French monarchy, the King is elected by God and through his coronation becomes God's "Lieutenant" on earth. The paintings and sculptures in the Chapel at Versailles evoke this idea in a cycle that starts at the nave and ends at the tribune where the King would be. Above the pillars of the nave are depicted angels bearing the instrument's of Christ's passion that lead to his death, a theme illustrated by the large bas-relief on the high altar; above, the altarpiece expresses the radiance of the resurrection, with the divine symbol of the triangle containing the name Iahve written in Hebrew in the midst of the rays. In the half-dome above the organ, Christ appears in the glory of the Resurrection, then in the vault is depicted God the Son and, finally, above the tribune can be seen the Descent of the Holy Spirit, the third person in the Holy Trinity, symbolised by a dove, which must inspire the actions of the king.

Antoine Coypel, central part of the chapel vault, *The Eternal Father in his glory bringing the world his promise of redemption.*

Corneille Van Clève, *Deposition*, bas-relief in gilded bronze for the high altar.

Organ (detail).

DONEC

THE OPERA ROYAL

GROUND FLOOR

From the outset, Versailles provided the setting for many events but until 1770 these always took place in provisional locations. It was at this time that the large auditorium, already planned by Louis XIV and under permanent consideration, was developed hastily for the marriage celebrations of the Dauphin, the future Louis XVI, to the Archduchess of Austria, Marie-Antoinette. This event led Gabriel, assisted by the stage engineer Arnoult, to design a modular auditorium which could be used for operas as well as balls and feasts, thanks to a mechanism that allowed the floor of the auditorium to be raised to the level of the stage. The dimensions of the auditorium, which then admitted more than a thousand spectators and which can still house six hundred today, make it the biggest court theatre in existence. However the auditorium only represents a quarter of the whole since the stage is as deep as the auditorium and the "below stage" areas for scene changes double its height. Its elegance stems from its harmonies of blue, white and gold, but above all from the colonnade and the mirror arcades of the last floor as well as the decompartmentalisation of the boxes: Gabriel thus avoided the "chicken coop" effect characteristic of Italian theatres as a result of tiered boxes stacked one on top of the other. Built from wood for the purposes of both economy and acoustics, the entire auditorium was vaulted by one of the best carpenters, Delanois, and enhanced with motifs carved by the great sculptor, Pajou. However, this auditorium was little used as it cost a crazy amount in candles and ordinary events were once again usually held in a provisional room. On 1 October 1789, the opera played host to a Banquet for the King's Bodyguards, an event that was considered to be very provocative and was highly relevant to the riot that forced the royal family to leave Versailles for good five days later. Re-used in 1837 for the inauguration of the museum created by Louis-Philippe, it temporarily housed the headquarters of the National Assembly in 1871, followed by the Senate from 1876 to 1879.

Bas-relief by Augustin Pajou.

Augustin Pajou, Cherubs symbolising the most famous operas: Pygmalion and Galatée.

THE HISTORY GALLERIES

FIRST FLOOR

After the revolution of 1830 which removed Charles X, the youngest brother of Louis XVI and the last of the Bourbons to reign, from power, his cousin, Louis-Philippe d'Orléans was proclaimed King of the French. By a decision taken in 1833, the new sovereign demonstrated his determination to break away from the *Ancien Régime* by removing from Versailles its status of royal residence and transforming it into a museum. A history enthusiast at a time when the discipline was becoming a veritable science, he decided to assemble there all the painted, carved, drawn and engraved images illustrating events or personalities from French history, right from its earliest days. To achieve this, he gathered items from royal, princely, private and institutional collections and supplemented these with thousands of copies and retrospective works commissioned from contemporary artists. He had his architect Nepveu organise everything. The architect went on to destroy many princely apartments, especially in the main two wings of the château where these history galleries are still in place today. Whilst, for Louis-Philippe, this museum, inaugurated in 1837 and devoted to "all of France's glories", reflected a political ambition – to reconcile the partisans of the various successive regimes since 1789 and hence assert his own legitimacy as King of all the French –, with more than 6000 paintings and 3000 sculptures, it remains the principal iconographic French history source.

THE BATTLE GALLERY

This gallery was created in 1837 by the architects Fontaine and Nepveu. 120 metres long, it occupies most of the South Wing, built in 1681 to house the princes of the royal family. Five beautiful apartments on the first floor and fourteen quarters for courtiers in the attic were destroyed to make way for this gallery commissioned by Louis-Philippe along with the 1830 room next to it.

In thirty-five large paintings and eighty-two busts, the Hall of Battles illustrates the exploits of the major military figures of France. The cycle begins with the depiction of Tolbiac, the founding victory of the French monarchy by Clovis in 496, and ends with that of Napoleon at Wagram in 1809. Other painters involved in fulfilling this prestigious official order were Eugène Delacroix, François Gérard and Horace Vernet.

Eugène Delacroix,
Saint Louis
at the Battle of Taillebourg,
21 July 1242.

THE CRUSADES ROOMS

Louis-Philippe created the Crusades Rooms to honour the former families of the nobility who had taken part in these expeditions to the Middle East. Their coats of arms can be seen painted on the ceilings of the five rooms. Originally, he had only planned the biggest of these rooms, which explains why the entire epic story of the eight crusades from the 11th to the 16th century is illustrated there. He had placed there, in the centre of the wall opposite the windows, the large cedar door from the hospital of Saint John of Jerusalem in Rhodes that the Ottoman Sultan had just given him, in 1836. The gothic décor of this door inspired all the decoration of the over-door panels, the chandeliers and the seats which make this suite of rooms one of the most beautiful examples of the "troubadour" style in vogue in the romantic period. It is reported that to meet this order, painters carried out meticulous research using ancient chronicles so that their retrospective works are not only of tremendous artistic quality but also of genuine historic interest.

Merry-Joseph Blondel,
Bohemond I, Prince of Antioch.

Below:
Merry-Joseph Blondel,
Acre (formerly Ptolemais),
handed over to Philip Augustus
and Richard the Lionheart
on 11 or 12 July 1191.

1100.
1096.
1096.
1096.
ÉTIENNE DE CHAMPAGNE
COMTE DE BLOIS
1096.
BOHÉMOND
PRINCE D'ANTIOCHE
1096.
ALAIN IV
1100.
GUILLAUME IX

THE 17th CENTURY ROOMS

In the North Wing, between the chapel and the opera, the 17th century rooms are an essential addition to any tour of the royal residence as they explain the creation of Versailles in terms of its historic and artistic context. They also portray the characters, events and scenes from the life of the court within the château throughout the long reign of Louis XIV.

Claude Lefebvre, *Jean-Baptiste Colbert, Controller-General of Finance.*

Carlo Maratta, *André Le Nôtre, Controller-General of the King's Gardens.*

French School, *Portrait of the Duke of Mortemart, father of Madame de Montespan.*

Nicolas Mignard (?), *Henrietta of England, Duchess of Orleans, sister-in-law of Louis XIV.*

THE 17th CENTURY ROOMS

Pierre Patel, *The château and gardens of Versailles in 1668.*

Charles Le Brun,
Henri de la Tour d'Auvergne,
Viscount of Turenne,
Marshal of France.

Right-hand page:
Henri Testelin, *Colbert introduces the members of the Royal Academy of Sciences created in 1666 to Louis XIV* (detail).
This painting reflects the sovereign's interest in the development of science.

THE REVOLUTION ROOMS

As one might expect, the Revolution does not enjoy a high profile at Versailles. For this period that was still painful at the time, Louis-Philippe restricted himself to purchasing a few portraits and creating the 1792 room. Located between the Coronation room and the Battle Gallery, this room recalls the victories of the French army as it defended the "country against the dangers it faced", including those at Valmy and Jemmapes; Louis-Philippe had himself portrayed there when he was a young lieutenant general. Today, four other rooms in the Chimay attic, above the Queen's rooms, illustrate the period. In addition to the unfinished canvas of the *Tennis Court Oath* (20 June 1789) as well as *Marat assassinated*, outstanding works by the painter David who was a member of the Convention, portraits of Revolution personalities as well as souvenirs of the tragic fate of the royal family are displayed there.

Jacques-Louis David,
The Tennis Court Oath in Versailles on 20 June 1789,
sketch.
Right-hand page: detail.

David's studio,
Jean-Paul Marat assassinated in his bath, 13 July 1793.

THE CONSULATE AND EMPIRE ROOMS

It is at Versailles that the story of the Napoleonic era is best depicted. It is told in thirty-one rooms distributed between the ground floor of the South Wing and the attics located above. When Louis-Philippe created his museum, there were still numerous and influential partisans of the Emperor, and the subject matter abounds as every artist felt moved to exalt Napoleon's glory. From his accession to power preceding his crowning ceremony on 2 December 1804 until his second abdication in 1815, every aspect of his reign is illustrated: military campaigns in Italy, Egypt and throughout Europe as far as Russia, diplomatic alliances, administrative reorganisation, the imperial family and dignitaries of the regime. As well as being of significant historic interest, the collection stands out for the artistic value of its works, produced by some of the greatest historic or portrait painters (Gros, Guérin, Girodet-Trioson, David, Regnault), topographic painters (Lejeune, Bagetti) and sculptors (Houdon, Boizot and Canova).

Claude Gautherot,
Napoleon harangues the second corps of the Grande Armée before attacking Augsburg.

Right-hand page:
Antoine-Jean Gros,
General Bonaparte at Arcola Bridge, 17 November 1796.

Jean-Baptiste Greuze,
Napoleon Bonaparte, First consul, in front of a view of Antwerp.

THE 19th CENTURY ROOMS

After the 1848 revolution forcing Louis-Philippe into exile, his successors carried on his work. These twenty-one 19th century rooms, located in the attic of the North Wing, illustrate the various periods of the century from the fall of Napoleon I until the Treaty of Versailles: the Restoration (from 1814 to 1830), the July Monarchy (from 1830 to 1848), the Second Empire (from 1852 to 1870), the birth of the Third Republic and the First World War (1914-1918). Military campaigns, scenes of court life, revolutionary days, series of portraits of princes by Gérard and Winterhalter, but also political personalities – such as Thiers, Gambetta and Clémenceau – and artistic personalities – such as Lamartine, Baudelaire, Stendhal, Hugo, Mallarmé, Debussy – extend and finish off the history galleries which make up a veritable album of France.

Maxime Dastugue, The novelist Honoré de Balzac.

Émile Halbon, The painter Eugène Delacroix.

Émile Deroy, The poet Charles Baudelaire.

Thomas Couture, The writer George Sand.

Anne-Louis Girodet de Roussy-Trioson, The diplomat and writer François René de Chateaubriand.

Léon Bonnat, The poet and novelist Victor Hugo.

Jean-François Raffaeli, The President of the Council Georges Clemenceau.

Pierre-Auguste Renoir, The poet Stéphane Mallarmé.

Louis-François Lejeune, *Charles X entering Paris on 6 June 1825*.

WEST SIDE

Since 1992, the gardens have been undergoing a re-planting programme and, following the devastating winter storm of December 1999, this work has been speeded up to such an extent that a number of areas have already regained their original appearance.
Viewers observing the gardens from the central window in the Hall of Mirrors have their eyes drawn from the *parterre d'Eau* or Water parterre (composed of two ornamental pools) to the horizon. Le Nôtre took pleasure in developing this original vista, that had existed prior to the reign of Louis XIV, and extending it by widening the Royal Avenue and having the Grand Canal dug.

THE *PARTERRE D'EAU* OR WATER PARTERRE

The two ornamental pools appear to be an extension of the château's façade. Altered several times, this ensemble only acquired its definitive appearance in 1685. The sculpted décor was then designed and overseen by Charles Le Brun: each pool is ringed with four reclining statues representing the rivers of France, as well as four nymphs and four groups of children. From 1687 to 1694, the Keller brothers, foundry owners, cast the models supplied by the sculptors (Tuby, Le Hongre, Regnaudin, Coysevox...) in bronze.

Coysevox, *The Marne*.
Right-hand page: Le Hongre, *The Seine*.

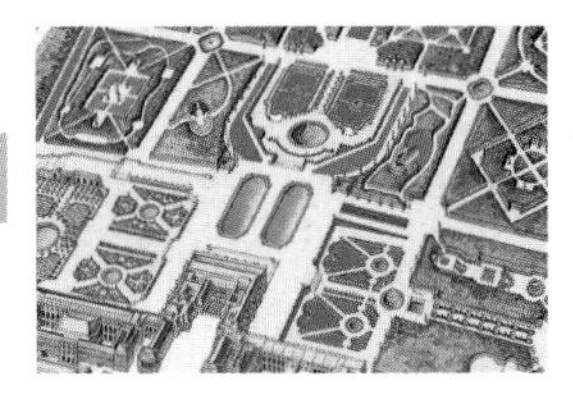

WEST SIDE

• THE *PARTERRE D'EAU* OR WATER PARTERRE

Colbert, *Orders and Regulations for the Buildings of Versailles, 24 October 1674*

"Inspect every pump twice a week. Make sure that nothing is missing and always have a second set of shafts, boards and bolts for all the devices... Constantly inspect all the fountains and count the number of workmen Denis [the head fountain master] *has according to his contract."*

Coysevox,
The Garonne.

Below:
Tuby, *The Rhône.*

The Water parterres cannot be viewed separately from the two fountains, known as the *"Combats des Animaux"* ("Animals in Combat"), finished in 1687, which frame the great stairway going down towards the Latona Basin, or the six allegorical statues: *L'Air* or Air (by Le Hongre), *Le Soir* or Evening (by Desjardins), *Le Midi* or Noon and *Le Point du Jour* or Daybreak (by G. Marsy), *Le Printemps* or Spring (by Magnier) and *L'Eau* or Water (by Le Gros), which formed part of Colbert's *grande commande* or "large order" for marble statues in 1674.

Houzeau, *Animals in combat, a bloodhound attacking a stag.*

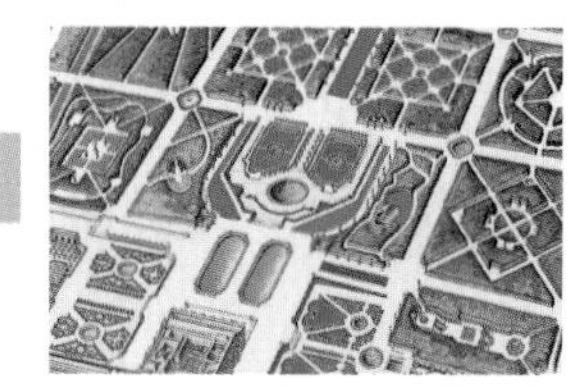

THE LATONA BASIN

Inspired by Ovid's *Metamorphoses*, the Latona Basin illustrates the legend of Apollo's mother and Diana protecting her children from the insults of the peasants of Lycia and asking Jupiter to avenge her. This he did by turning them into frogs or lizards.

The central marble work by the Marsy brothers depicting Latona and her children was originally located, in 1670, on a rock. It was surrounded by six half-submerged frogs, and twenty-four more frogs were positioned outside the basin, on the raised lawn. At that time, the goddess looked towards the château.

This arrangement was modified by Jules Hardouin-Mansart between 1687 and 1689. The rock made way for a concentric marble plinth and the Latona group now faces the Grand Canal. The Latona Basin is extended by a parterre where the two lizard fountains are located.

• THE ROYAL AVENUE

Also known as the *"Tapis Vert"* or "Green Carpet" due to the lawn running down the middle, the Royal Avenue is 335 metres long and 40 metres wide. The original layout dates back to Louis XIII, but Le Nôtre had it enlarged and enhanced with twelve statues and twelve vases (placed in symmetrical pairs). The majority of these are royal works sent by students of the Academy of France in Rome in the 17th century. On either side of the avenue, pathways give access to the groves that visitors to the gardens gradually discover as they go.

WEST SIDE

THE APOLLO BASIN AND THE GRAND CANAL

A basin (known as the "Basin of Swans") existed at this spot as early as 1636, under Louis XIII. Louis XIV had it enlarged and adorned with the sumptuous and famous ensemble in gilded lead representing *Apollo on his chariot*, a work by Tuby based on a drawing by Le Brun. Tuby produced this monumental group between 1668 and 1670 at the Gobelin factory. It was then transported to Versailles before being put into position and gilded the following year.
Work on the Grand Canal, which is next, lasted eleven years (from 1668 to 1679). It provided the setting for numerous water festivals and numerous small boats sailed on it. From 1669, Louis XIV had miniature boats and vessels brought in. In 1674, the Republic of Venice sent the king two gondolas and four gondoliers, who were housed in a group of buildings at the head of the canal, known as Little Venice.

Louis XIV, *The Manner of Presenting the Gardens of Versailles*

"Walk down to Apollo, and pause to contemplate the figures, the vases along the Royal Avenue, Latona and the château; one can also see the canal. If one wishes to see the Menagerie and Trianon on the same day, this should be done before seeing the other fountains."

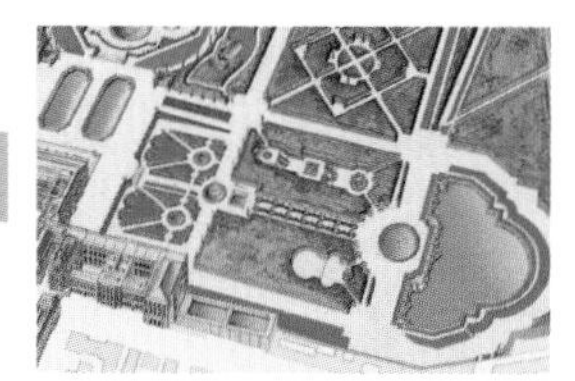

NORTH SIDE

In the northern part of the gardens, the water theme dominates, probably because the naturally sloping terrain was ideal for accommodating numerous water features. But the Grotto of Thetis was also located nearby until 1684. At the time, this attracted many visitors due to the variety of its fountains and the beauty of its interior décor.
The same principal as is employed along the east-west axis – a central avenue, opening up the view, and lined with groves surrounded by arbours – is used here. Steps, a Pyramid fountain (equivalent to the Latona Basin), a Water Avenue (which extends the vista in the same way as the Royal Avenue) and the Dragon Basin (the theme of which can be compared with the Baths of Apollo), culminating in a vast pool of water: the Neptune Basin.

Matthieu Lespagnandelle, *Phlegmatic Man*.

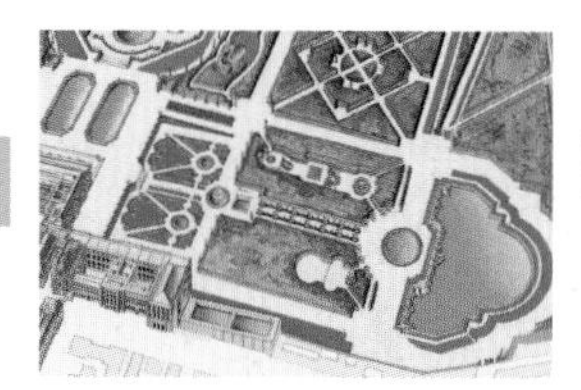

NORTH SIDE

THE *PARTERRE DU NORD* OR NORTH FLOWERBED

From the central terrace and the Water parterre, visitors go down a few steps framed by two bronze sculptures: *The Chaste Venus*, by Coysevox, and *The Knifegrinder*, by Foggini, towards the North parterre designed in 1664. On either side of the central avenue are the two *"Bassins des Couronnes"* or "Crown Basins" in which lead tritons and mermaids – works by Tuby and Le Hongre – can be seen swimming. The North parterre is surrounded by eighteen sculptures, fifteen of which belong to the *grande commande* or "large order" of 1674. Its iconographic design, drawn up by Charles Le Brun, illustrates the myth of Apollo and his life-giving and influential race around the earth; the statues were arranged in fours: the four continents, the four seasons, the four temperaments... but the perpetual changes that were made to the way the gardens were laid out soon led to these ensembles being dispersed.

From Coysevox, *The Chaste Venus.*
Foggini, *The Knifegrinder.*

NORTH SIDE

THE PYRAMID FOUNTAIN

A work by Girardon based on a drawing by Le Brun, the Pyramid Fountain took three years to complete. It is made up of four superimposed marble basins held up by lead tritons, dolphins and crayfish.

THE FOUNTAIN OF NYMPHS' BASIN

Fed by water from the Pyramid fountain, the cascade, known as the *Bain des Nymphes de Diane* or Baths of Diana's Nymphs, is adorned with bas-reliefs, the most well-known of which on the supporting wall is a lead work by Girardon (1668-1670) that was previously gilded. The others are by Le Gros, Le Hongre and Magnier.

THE WATER AVENUE

According to his brother Charles (the famous fable writer), it was Claude Perrault (the architect) who designed this avenue, also known as the *allée des Marmousets* or Children's Alley. It is punctuated by twenty-two bronze sculptures supporting Languedoc marble basins.

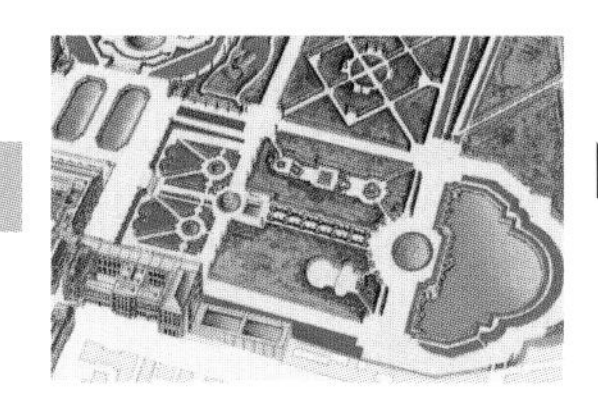

NORTH SIDE

THE DRAGON BASIN

The Water Avenue culminates with a half-moon at the Dragon Basin, depicting one of the episodes in the legend of Apollo: the Python (killed by the young Apollo's arrow) is surrounded by dolphins and cupids armed with bow and arrows, riding on swans. The main water jet rises up twenty-seven metres. On either side of this basin, alleys lead to two recently restored groves: to the east is the *Bosquet de la France Triomphante* or Triumphant France Grove and to the west the *Bosquet des Trois-Fontaines* or Three Fountains Grove.

THE NEPTUNE BASIN

It was Le Nôtre who oversaw construction of the Neptune Basin between 1679 and 1681, at the time known as the "Pool under the Dragon" or "Fir pool". Jacques-Ange Gabriel altered it slightly in 1736 and, in 1740, the three groups of sculptures were put into place: *Neptune and Amphitrite* by L.-S. Adam, *Proteus* by Bouchardon and *Ocean*, by J.-B. Lemoyne. The new basin, inaugurated by Louis XV, was admired for the number, size and variety of fountains, creating an extraordinary hydraulic ensemble.

SOUTH SIDE

THE *PARTERRE DU SUD* OR SOUTH FLOWERBED

The best view of this is probably to be gained from the Queen's Suite, on the first floor of the château. Previously named the parterre des Fleurs (Flower parterre) or parterre de l'Amour (Love parterre) it is located below the Orangery built by Jules Hardouin-Mansart. It is reached via a set of steps flanked by two of the oldest sculptures in the park: "Les Enfants aux sphinx" or "Children with Sphinxes". The bronze children were modelled by Sarazin, cast by Duval in 1668 and placed on marble sphinxes, carved by Lerambert.

Van Clève, *Ariadne sleeping*, copy of classical sculpture.

SOUTH SIDE

• THE ORANGERY

Built by Jules Hardouin-Mansart between 1684 and 1686 to replace the small orangery erected by Le Vau in 1663, it comprises a central vaulted gallery, 155 metres long, extended by two side galleries beneath the Great 100-Step Staircases. Light comes in through large, arched windows. The Orangery parterre extends over three hectares; under Louis XIV it was adorned with a few sculptures which are now in the Louvre. Made up of four areas of lawn and a circular pool, in the summer it boasts 1,055 trees in tubs (palm trees, oleanders, pomegranate trees, eugenia, orange trees, etc.) which are housed inside the Orangery in the winter.
Beyond the Orangery parterre, on the other side of the *Route de Saint-Cyr*, lies the Swiss Pool. Digging began in 1678 and was completed in 1688. It is 682 metres long and 234 wide, covering an area of 16 hectares (twice the size of the *Place de la Concorde* in Paris).

The Orangery parterre with the Swiss Pool in the background.

The Orangery parterre has had its original lines designed by Le Nôtre restored, along with the ochre colour of the door and window frames.

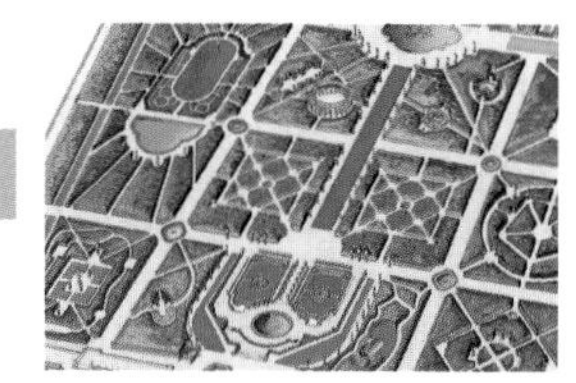

THE BACCHUS AND SATURN AVENUE

Under the reign of Louis XIV, the gardens at Versailles had fifteen *bosquets* or groves, in other words spaces that were hidden from view by arbours and closed off with gates. They acted as a counterpoint to the rigid regularity of the overall layout of the gardens, their décor and shape differed and their overall effect was to surprise visitors through their diversity. The majority of them were created by Le Nôtre, but some were modified by Jules Hardouin-Mansart. These charming green spaces, havens of fantasy, abound with fountains and sculptures. Festivities, dancing, music, theatre and meals were all held there. However, due to the fact that they were expensive and difficult to maintain, some groves deteriorated rapidly and were closed from as early as the 18th century. One of the most famous, the Labyrinth, was destroyed when the gardens were replanted in the period 1775-1776, others such as the Baths of Apollo were transformed in the highly fashionable Anglo-Chinese style under the reign of Louis XVI and Marie-Antoinette. In the 19th century, under the reign of Louis XVIII, the Royal Island was filled in and became the King's Garden, planted with rare and exotic trees.

Parallel to the Royal Avenue, two main axes give access to the North and South Groves (*Bosquet du Nord* and *Bosquet du Sud*). To the south is the Bacchus (autumn) and Saturn (winter) avenue punctuated by two basins with gilded lead statues in their centre, works by the Marsy brothers and Girardon. With their symmetrical counterparts in the north, these symbolise the four seasons.

• THE QUEEN'S GROVE

This grove replaced the famous Labyrinth which illustrated thirty-nine Aesop's fables at each of its crossroads by lead fountains painted *au naturel* depicting animals. Constructed in 1669 from an idea by Charles Perrault, it was destroyed when the gardens were replanted in the period 1775-1776, to be replaced by the Queen's Grove. The current sculptures were put in place at the end of the 19th century.

Venus Medicis, bronze cast by the Keller brothers.

Jean Cotelle (The Younger), *The entrance to the Labyrinth in the Gardens of Versailles with the Cabinet of Birds and the statues of Aesop and Ariadne* (in the foreground, nymphs taking birds).

Colbert, *Orders and Regulations for the Buildings of Versailles, 30 September 1672*

"In the gardens: as soon as possible have Berthier, the rock mason, set up two or three workshops to restore all the rockwork. [...] Examine and repair the rockwork such that it is fully restored, using either cement or brass wire: use that which is the most solid. Bring in the smelter, and have him carefully inspect all taps, valves, fittings and all other copper works, to renovate everything."

• THE BALLROOM GROVE

Designed by Le Nôtre between 1680 and 1683, the Ballroom is also known as the *Bosquet des Rocailles* (Rockery grove) due to the millstones and shells brought back from the African coasts and Madagascar over which the water flows. In the middle, a marble "island", easily accessible, was used for dancing, something Louis XIV was famous for. The musicians positioned themselves above the waterfall and the spectators would sit opposite, in an amphitheatre with grass-covered terraces.

• THE DAUPHIN'S GROVE AND THE GIRANDOLE GROVE

The Dauphin's Grove and the Girandole's Grove, the restoration of which was completed in 2000, replace to the north and the south the former zigzag patterns planted under Louis XVI. Each of these groves is decorated with items ordered by Superintendent Fouquet for his château de Vaux-le-Vicomte and produced in Rome based on Poussin's models. At the end of the 17th century, the sculptor Théodon completed this series of sculptures, dedicated to the seasons or mythological divinities.

Théodon, *Ceres*.

On the left:
from Poussin,
Reaper
and *Pomona*.

• THE CHESTNUT GROVE

Arranged between 1680 and 1683, it was then known as the *Galerie des Antiques* (Classical Gallery) or *Galerie d'Eau* (Water Gallery) and comprised a central avenue bordered with orange trees, pruned yew trees, pools and water jets. Around this avenue there were twenty-four Classical statues.
Entirely re-designed in 1704, this grove then became the *Salle des Marronniers* or Chestnut Grove, adorned with eight Classical busts and two statues. The only aspects of the original décor to survive are the two round basins located at each end.

Septime Sévère,
17th century copy,
from a classical
sculpture.

On the left:
Meleagrus,
classical sculpture
restored in
the 17th century.

THE KING'S GARDEN

The Mirror Basin was at the edge of a large pond known as the *Île d'Amour* (Love Island) or *Île Royale* (Royal Island) (1674) on which model warships were tested out. It was not maintained during the period of the Revolution and was removed in 1817 by the architect Dufour, on the orders of Louis XVIII, to be replaced with the King's Garden. This enclosed, English-style garden was planted with superb plant species most of which were subsequently wiped out by the winter storm of 1999. All that now remains of the original design is the Mirror Basin.

• THE COLONNADE GROVE

Built from 1685 by Jules Hardouin-Mansart, the Colonnade replaced a grove created by Le Nôtre in 1679: the *Bosquet des Sources* or Grove of Springs. This peristyle has a diameter of thirty-two metres; thirty-two Ionic order marble columns connected to thirty-two Languedoc marble pilasters, support arcades and a white marble cornice, itself topped by thirty-two urns. The triangular tympanums between the arches are decorated with bas-reliefs depicting children. The archstones are adorned with nymphs and naiads. In the centre, a circular marble plinth acts as a pedestal for the famous composition executed between 1678 and 1699 by Girardon: *Pluto abducting Proserpine* (a cast replaced the original, now in storage).

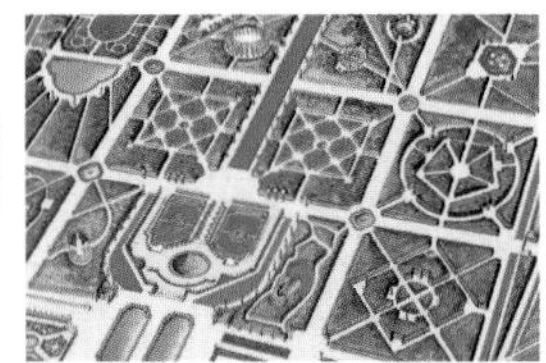

THE FLORA AND CERES AVENUE

Symmetrical to the Bachus and Saturn Basins, the Flora and Ceres Basins symbolise the summer and the spring respectively. Flora, half-naked, is resting on a bed of flowers, also surrounded by Cupids weaving garlands. The sculptor produced these between 1672 and 1677. Ceres, sickle in hand, surrounded by Cupids is reclining on the ground strewn with ears of wheat. This work is by the sculptor Regnaudin.

THE AVENUES AND GROVES

THE DOME GROVE

Frequently re-designed, the name of this grove has been changed each time modifications have been made. Created by Le Nôtre in 1675, it was then known as the *bosquet de la Renommée* or Fame grove, in the period 1677-1678, due to the statue of *la Renommée* (or Fame) placed in the centre of the basin at this time with a fountain coming out of her trumpet. Between 1684 and 1704, the sculpted groups from the Apollo baths were placed there, hence the name Baths of Apollo and Baths during that period. In 1677, Jules Hardouin-Mansart had built two white marble pavilions surmounted by domes, giving it its current name, although these constructions were destroyed in 1820.

Simoneau the Younger, *The Dome Grove in 1688.*

THE ENCELADUS BASIN

The Enceladus Fountain was produced in lead by Gaspard Marsy between 1675 and 1677. The subject is borrowed from history from the fall of the Titans, buried beneath the rocks of Mount Olympus that they wanted to climb in defiance of Jupiter's ban on doing so. The sculptor represented a giant half-engulfed beneath the rocks, battling against death. This grove was restored between 1992 and 1998.

Jean Cotelle (The Younger), *View of the Enceladus Fountain with Lycaon's feast.*

• THE OBELISK

The Obelisk Fountain was built by Jules Hardouin-Mansart in 1704 at the location of the former *salle des Festins* (Feast room) or *salle du Conseil* (Council room), designed by Le Nôtre in 1671. The lead décor was then used as ornamentation for the basins in the Grand Trianon garden.

• THE CHILDREN'S ISLAND

On the north side of the gardens, between the *Rond vert* or Green Circle (formerly known as the *bosquet du Théâtre d'eau* or Water Theatre grove) and the Star (formerly the *bosquet de la Montagne d'eau* or Water Mountain Grove), away from the busy avenues, is hidden a circular basin from the middle of which rises a rock. This is the Children's Island, a masterpiece of purity created by Hardy dating back to 1710. On the rock there are six children playing with flowers, whilst two others are frolicking in the water.

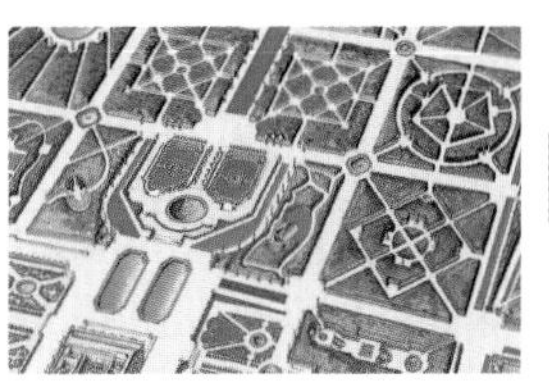

THE BATHS OF APOLLO

Here, a grove, known as *le Marais* (the Marsh), was created during the reign of Louis XIV, between 1670 and 1673, on the instigation of Madame de Montespan. In 1704, Jules Hardouin-Mansart designed a new grove for this location to receive the *Chevaux du Soleil* or Sun Horses (work by Guérin and the Marsy brothers) and *Apollon servi par les Nymphes* or Apollo tended by Nymphs (work by Girardon and Regnaudin). This ensemble was sculpted between 1664 and 1672 to adorn the famous Grotto of Thetis, and when the latter was destroyed to make way for the north wing of the Château, it was transferred to the Dome Grove.
Hardouin-Mansart designed this location therefore to showcase his particularly remarkable works. They were sheltered under gilded lead baldaquins and placed on a plinth along the edge of a basin.
This arrangement remained in place until 1776. Then, a year after the order given by Louis XVI to replant the grounds, the painter Hubert Robert was asked to come up with a new design. The grove he came up with, completed in 1778, is in the then highly fashionable Anglo-Chinese style. It is his design that still remains to this day.

Francois Girardon and Thomas Regnaudin, *Apollo tended by the nymphs of Thetis.*

Marsy brothers, *Sun Horses.*

THE THREE FOUNTAINS GROVE

Created by le Nôtre in 1677, this grove is the only one mentioned on an old map as being *"the King's idea"*. It comprises three terraces, each of which presents a different basin. It was magnificently restored in 2005 to fully reveal the splendour of the composition and water jets commissioned by the sovereign: in the lower basin, the jets of water form fleurs de lys, in the centre, vertical lances and an arc of water and, finally the upper basin comprises a column of water formed by 140 jets; it is actually this imposing column that feeds the lower basins. Although hidden by trelliswork, the grove had been designed in such a way that the ageing king could go there in his wheelchair and move from one place to another on lawned access ramps.

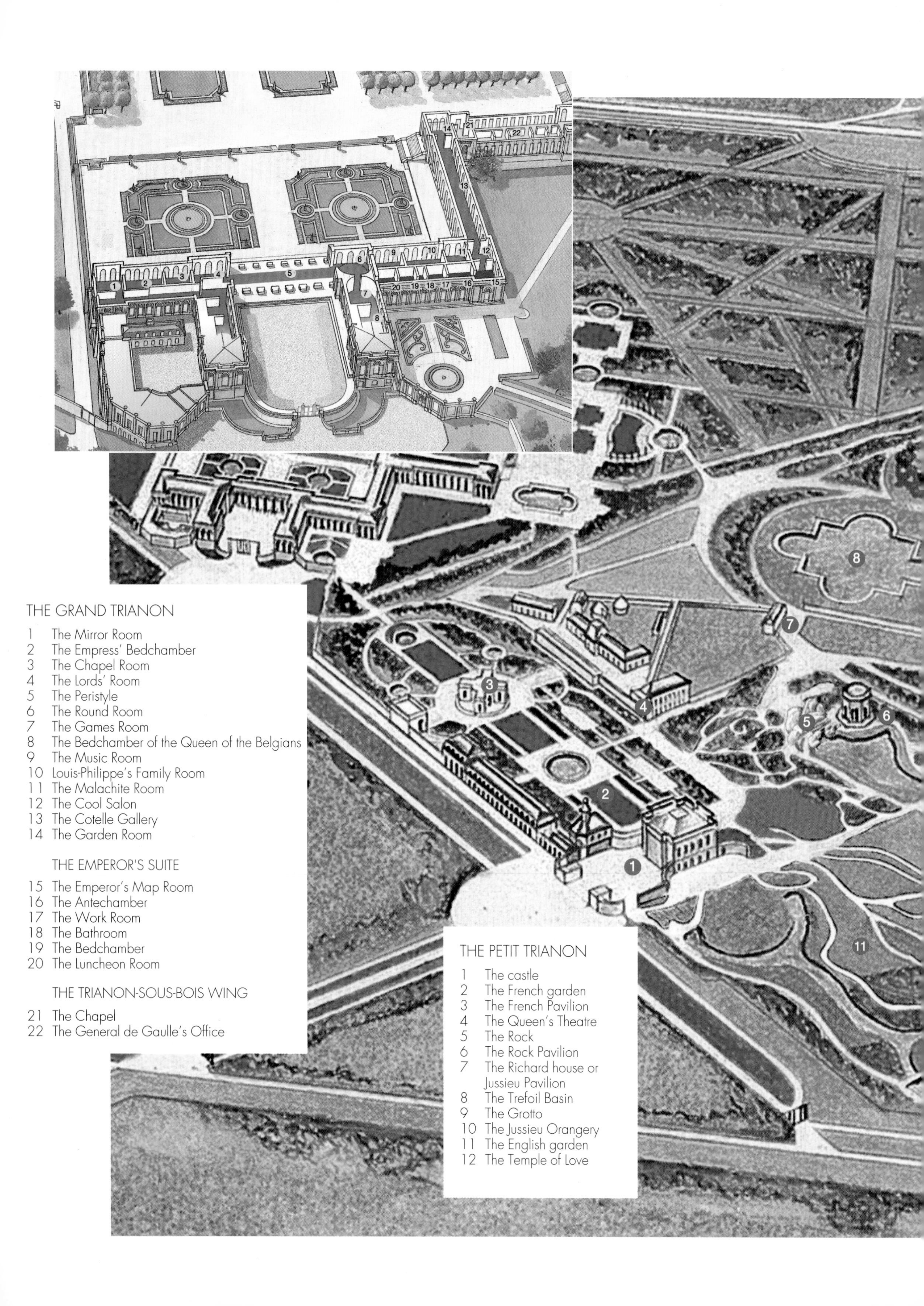

THE GRAND TRIANON

1 The Mirror Room
2 The Empress' Bedchamber
3 The Chapel Room
4 The Lords' Room
5 The Peristyle
6 The Round Room
7 The Games Room
8 The Bedchamber of the Queen of the Belgians
9 The Music Room
10 Louis-Philippe's Family Room
11 The Malachite Room
12 The Cool Salon
13 The Cotelle Gallery
14 The Garden Room

THE EMPEROR'S SUITE

15 The Emperor's Map Room
16 The Antechamber
17 The Work Room
18 The Bathroom
19 The Bedchamber
20 The Luncheon Room

THE TRIANON-SOUS-BOIS WING

21 The Chapel
22 The General de Gaulle's Office

THE PETIT TRIANON

1 The castle
2 The French garden
3 The French Pavilion
4 The Queen's Theatre
5 The Rock
6 The Rock Pavilion
7 The Richard house or Jussieu Pavilion
8 The Trefoil Basin
9 The Grotto
10 The Jussieu Orangery
11 The English garden
12 The Temple of Love

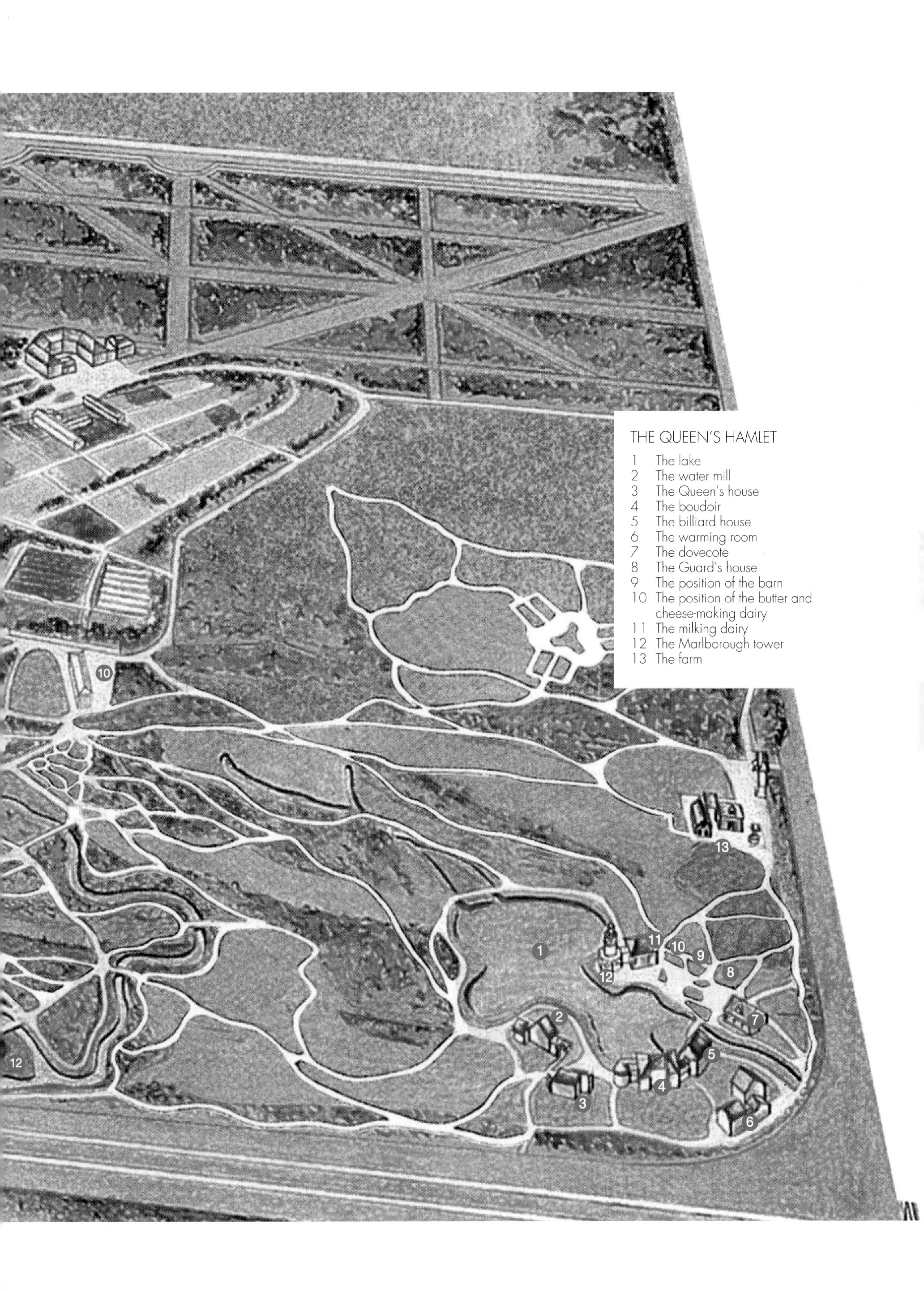
THE QUEEN'S HAMLET
1 The lake
2 The water mill
3 The Queen's house
4 The boudoir
5 The billiard house
6 The warming room
7 The dovecote
8 The Guard's house
9 The position of the barn
10 The position of the butter and cheese-making dairy
11 The milking dairy
12 The Marlborough tower
13 The farm

THE GRAND TRIANON

The Grand Trianon is located to the north-west of the château de Versailles, on the site of a former village purchased by the sovereign. Unique in terms of the originality of its architecture, it may be said to be the work of Hardouin-Mansart and the king himself as Louis XIV closely oversaw its development in 1687. During this period, Versailles was crowded with courtiers. The Trianon was to be a place to rest, a private space, reserved for concerts, celebrations and even light meals, to which Louis XIV wanted to invite only the ladies of the court; later it was for family use. At this time, the Grand Trianon was known as the Marble Trianon, due to the Rance columns of the portico and the pink Languedoc pilasters, adorned with white Carrara capitals giving emphasis to all the façades, and also in contrast to a first house known as the Porcelain Trianon, the existence of which was short-lived. The Trianon is the Floral palace: from every room there is a view onto the gardens, which here are entirely given over to flowers, with a large number of varieties selected for their colours as well as their scents: "The tuberoses cause us to abandon the Trianon every evening", writes Madame de Maintenon in a letter of 8 August 1689, "men and women feel ill, overwhelmed by the scents." And all the décors, paintings and carvings on the panelling are inspired by this floral motif.

• THE MIRROR ROOM

With its wonderful view over the Grand Canal and its décor of mirrors, this room is the most beautiful in the south wing. It was the last room in the apartments that Louis XIV occupied in this part of the château between 1691 and 1703, in which he held counsel. Like the majority of the areas in the Trianon, it has retained its original décor but not the furniture, which was sold during the Revolution and later replaced by Napoleon. From 1810 to 1814, it was used as the State Cabinet of Archduchess Marie-Louise, the great-niece of Marie-Antoinette and the emperor's second wife.

• THE EMPRESS' BEDCHAMBER

This room met with the same fate as the previous one. The bedchamber of Louis XIV, it has retained its décor characterised by the presence of Corinthian columns dividing the room and the wonderfully carved mosaics of the panelling. Later it was the Empress Marie-Louise's bedchamber and re-furnished for her as it is seen today; the only exception is the bed, which was Napoleon's bed in the Tuileries Palace and the one in which his successor Louis XVIII, Louis XVI's brother, died in 1825, before finally being brought here for the last occupant of the room, Queen Marie-Amélie, King Louis-Philippe's wife.

The Hall of Mirrors has regained its furnishings delivered by Jacob-Desmalter. Opposite, detail of an armchair. On the right, console.

• THE LORDS' ROOM

This room has retained its original name, from the time the entire south wing was used for serving light meals. It then became the king's first antechamber, followed by that of the empress. The great table was produced in 1823 by Félix Rémond, its top being of a single piece of teak with a diameter of 2.77 m.

• THE PERISTYLE

Incorrectly called the peristyle – but the name dates from the time of Louis XIV – this portico cutting through the centre of the building gives the Grand Trianon its transparency and hence originality, allowing people to move imperceptibly from the courtyard to the gardens.

• THE ROUND ROOM

This hall gave access to the first apartment occupied by Louis XIV for just three years, from 1688 to 1691. Its décor of Corinthian columns as well as its marble paving and paintings date from this period. To the right of the fireplace, a wooden swing door conceals the staircase used by musicians to access the gallery leading to the following room, in which the king's supper was taken.

• LOUIS-PHILIPPE'S FAMILY ROOM

This large room was created by Louis-Philippe from two existing rooms. In the evenings, the king and his family, who liked to stay at the Trianon, gathered in this room furnished in the spirit of the time: games and work tables, lined seats and sofas covered with yellow purl with a blue motif.

• THE MALACHITE ROOM

This grand room of the Emperor took its name from the malachite gifts given by Tsar Alexander I to Napoleon that were placed there.

• THE EMPEROR'S MAP ROOM

Originally this cabinet opened onto the *bosquet des Sources* or Grove of Springs, a small wood, criss-crossed by streams meandering through the trees and the last creation of Le Nôtre that disappeared under Louis XVI. It then led to Madame de Maintenon's apartment and views of the gardens at Versailles, in which an elderly Louis XIV is depicted in a wheel chair, are embedded in its panelling. In 1810, Napoleon turned this room into his map room and used the neighbouring suite of rooms as his private apartments.

Pierre Denis Martin, *View of the Apollo Basin and the Grand Canal in Versailles in 1713* (detail), in the foreground: Louis XIV taking a stroll.

• THE EMPEROR'S BEDCHAMBER

The Emperor's bedchamber, one of the five rooms in his private apartments, had been decorated under Louis XV with the panelling that still exists to this day. It was re-furnished in its Empire style and the beautiful "lemon-wood" moire fabrics with lilac and silver brocade border, which had been woven in Lyons for Joséphine in 1807 and which were re-used here for Napoleon in 1809. It was in December of the same year that Napoleon stayed in this private suite for the first time, just after his divorce from Josephine. The latter's daughter, Queen Hortense, recounted, however, that the Emperor received them on the 25th of the same month: "[He] went to Trianon and asked us to visit him. I accompanied my mother. This meeting was touching. The Emperor wanted her to stay to dine. As usual, he sat opposite her. Nothing seemed to have changed [...] There was a deep silence. My mother couldn't eat anything else and I saw that she was ready to faint. The Emperor wiped his eyes two or three times without saying a word and we left immediately after dinner."

• THE BEDCHAMBER OF THE QUEEN OF THE BELGIANS

The right wing, which looks over the Courtyard of Honour, housed a theatre under Louis XIV, then, under Louis XV, reception rooms (games room, dining room and a buffet room). Louis-Philippe transformed it to create apartments for his son-in-law and his daughter Louise-Marie of Orleans, the King and Queen of the Belgians. Amongst the items of furniture brought from the Tuileries Palace was the Empress Josephine's bed.

• THE GAMES ROOM

Although annexed to the young Belgian sovereigns' apartments, Louis XV's former games room has retained its curved appearance, panellings as well as its beautiful purple breccia fireplace.

• THE COTELLE GALLERY

Judiciously built to shelter the Trianon flower beds from the rigours of winter, this gallery has eleven French windows on the south side, and only five windows on the north side. It is adorned with twenty-four paintings (twenty-one of which are by Jean Cotelle) which depict the groves at Versailles and Trianon at the time they were commissioned, in 1687, precious illustrations of the gardens as they were during the 17th century. Originally, the recesses contained sofas and Louis-Philippe had the two Languedoc marble wine coolers from Louis XV's sideboards put there.
It was here, on 4 June 1920, that the peace treaty with Hungary was signed, putting an end to the First World War.

Jean Cotelle (The Younger) , *View of the Trianon parterres with Flora and Zephyr.*

• THE GARDEN ROOM

At the end of the Cotelle Gallery, the Garden Room looks out over the Trianon's *salle des Marroniers* or Chestnut Grove and, beyond the upper parterre, onto the transverse arm of the Grand Canal. Under Louis XIV, there was a table for the game of portique (similar to roulette) placed in the centre of this room, which was subsequently replaced by a billiard table.

THE TRIANON-SOUS-BOIS WING

Twenty years after its construction, the Trianon had grown too small to accommodate all of Louis XIV's family. To satisfy the king, Jules Hardouin-Mansart, shortly before his death in 1708, built this Trianon-sous-Bois wing, the sobriety and elegance of which heralded the style of the 18th century. This section of the building, the only part with an upstairs, offers a set of apartments that were initially used by Madame Palatine, the king's sister-in-law, and her children.

• THE CHAPEL

Alongside the garden room and its portique game, the chapel was created by Louis-Philippe on the site of Louis XIV's Billiard room for the marriage of his second daughter, Princess Marie, to Duke Alexander of Würtemberg, on 17 October 1837.

• THE GENERAL'S OFFICE

Between 1962 and 1967, General de Gaulle had the Trianon-sous-Bois wing restored to accommodate presidents of the French Republic. In particular, the general's office is there.

THE PETIT TRIANON

Madame de Pompadour, who wanted to "relieve the king's boredom" – she was no longer his mistress but remained a friend –, was the instigator of this small château built by Gabriel between 1763 and 1768 close to the botanic garden and the new menagerie, as Louis XV was interested in the sciences. To please the marchioness who always liked to keep up with the latest fashions, the king's architect broke away from the rococo style of aesthetics and adopted a cubic form for the building with very pure lines in keeping with the new, so-called "Greek" style that was in vogue. Its simplicity is only an outward appearance as each of the façades is different, treated differently depending on the space it looks onto: the courtyard, the French garden with its pretty pavilion, the botanic garden and the flower garden. Inside one finds the same modern style. Madame de Pompadou did not live to see the château completed and today it is mainly Marie-Antoinette's memory that remains there: in 1774, Louis XVI gave the Trianon estate to his wife who was able to live her life there removed – too far-removed for some people – from the Court.

• THE PUBLIC SALON

Devoted to games, conversation and music, this room with its sober décor gives an accurate impression of the quest for pleasure characteristic of the 18th century. The over-door paintings inspired by Ovid's *Metamorphoses* illustrate the importance given to flowers at the Trianon. They depict: *Clytia* transformed into a sunflower and *Apollo and Hyacinth*, by Nicolas-René Jollain; *Adonis changed into an anemone* and *Narcissus changed into the flower of the same name*, by Nicolas-Bernard Lépicié. The ostrich egg placed in the centre of the pedestal table comes from the collections of Madame Adelaide, one of Louis XV's daughters.

As told by Madame Campan, her first chambermaid: "She [Marie-Antoinette] had a real taste for her retirement at the Trianon; she went there alone, followed by a footman, but found staff there ready to receive her: a caretaker and his wife, who then acted as her chambermaid." She did, however, invite her close friends and family there; the king was happy to drop in; hence this room was a gathering place for meetings, music and games. Although the château was largely re-furnished for the Queen, the majority of its décor remained that chosen by Louis XV and Madame de Pompadour: for example, the magnificent panelling carved with the monogram of Louis XV with white-painted rose petals on a soft water-green background.

On the right: Élisabeth Vigée-Lebrun, *Marie-Antoinette with a rose*.

THE QUEEN'S THEATRE

Whereas the Versailles opera is a court theatre, the small auditorium at Trianon is a society theatre, as existed at the time in many country residences where, to pass the time, manor owners and their guests put on plays and operas. In her childhood in Vienna, Marie-Antoinette grew used to these informal events. She wanted to do the same thing for her family, princes of the royal family and a few rare friends. In 1780, therefore, on her orders, Richard Mique built this theatre with its severe exterior and starkly contrasting refined interior which, through its blue, white and gold harmonies brings to mind the Versailles opera, only smaller as here around hundred people could be admitted: servants on the parterre and guests upstairs behind the boxes fitted with bars. But the greatest luxury does not lie in the wooden auditorium painted in false white veined marble and adorned with pasteboard sculptures but in the machinery used for scene changes, which has fortunately been preserved. At the Trianon, plays by fashionable authors were staged – Sedaine, Rousseau – and entire operas were sung in which, everyone agreed, the queen was very good.

THE FRENCH PAVILION

This building was called the "French" pavilion due to its location in the middle of one of these formal gardens that people has started referring to as "French" in contrast with the emerging fashion for English gardens. Built by Gabriel in 1750, it was one of Louis XV's first creations at Trianon, this estate of which he was very fond from his childhood. It comprises a vast circular salon flanked by four small rooms used as a boudoir, a *rechauffoir* or room for warming up food, a kitchen and a wardrobe. Accompanied by the Marchioness de Pompadour the king often came here to rest or listen to music after a stroll through the botanic gardens or a light meal in the neighbouring *Salon Frais* (Cool Salon).

• ROCK PAVILION

Overlooking the lake, this charming octagonal music pavilion was built by Richard Mique in 1777. The outside is decorated with sculptures by Deschamps: a frieze of a garland of fruits formerly coloured, pediments depicting the pleasures of hunting and gardening, window imposts symbolising the four seasons. Inside, the circular room is paved with a marble mosaic and its walls are adorned with fine arabesques.

Claude-Louis Châtelet, *Illumination of the Rock Pavilion and the rock on 3 August 1781*, in honour of Joseph II, brother of Marie-Antoinette.

• THE TEMPLE OF LOVE

This Temple of Love that the queen could see from her bedchamber at the Petit Trianon was built by Richard Mique in 1778 in a neoclassical style. Entirely in marble, this precious building is above all remarkable for the quality of its Deschamps sculptures adoring its Corinthian capitals, its friezes and the inside of its dome. This exceptional quality can be explained by the fact that it was intended to house a recognised masterpiece of French sculpture, *Cupid making a bow out of the club of Hercules* by Bouchardon. The original, today in the Louvre, was replaced by a copy by Mouchy, another great sculptor of the 18th century.

THE QUEEN'S HAMLET

This village with its thatched roofs, inspired by the hamlets of Normandy, was created by Mique between 1783 and 1785. Fashion demanded a "return to nature" and the queen yielded to this vogue. There were twelve houses. Facing the artificial lake, the most important construction was the queen's cottage linked to the Billiard house by a gallery of wood, from where the Lady of the Trianon could watch the work in the fields. Behind their rustic appearance, the interiors were highly sophisticated (furniture by Riesener and Jacob, Sèvres porcelain). The Malborough tower overlooks the fishing weir as well as the milking dairy used for cheese making. Today, the water mill, the rechauffoir (or warming room), the boudoir, the dovecote and the guard's house remain of this fantasy, as well as, slightly separate, the farm which was tended by a couple of peasants from the Touraine. There was a barn (also used as a ballroom) and a butter and cheese-making dairy, of which only traces of the foundations remain.

The Malborough tower, the basement of which contains a fish weir.

The water mill.

Next pages:
The Queen's house consists of two buildings linked by a gallery: on the left the billiard house and on the right the Queen's house proper. Behind is the *"réchauffoir"* or warming room.

The farm, on the left, the farm courtyard and, above, the Guard's House.

Crédits photographiques :

Artlys/Bréjat H. : p. 24-25, 27, 28, 32, 68-69, 84, 95 ; Artlys/Burnier É. : p. 88, 131 ; Artlys/Février A. : p. 7, 42, 70, 94, 114, 116-117, 120-121, 122, 124, 128, 129, 139, 140, 142, 143, 147, 149, 181 ; Artlys/Girard J. : p. 21, 115, 117, 130, 133, 141, 142, 143, 145, 146, 150, 151, 153, 182, 183 ; Artlys/Varga J.-C. : p. 65, 75, 81 ; RMN : 16-17, 22, 46-47, 53, 56, 60, 61, 80, 100, 109, 180 ; RMN/Arnaudet D. : p. 6, 7, 44, 54, 58, 108, 110, 113, 116, 128, 134, 135, 184 ; RMN/Arnaudet D. et Blot G. : p. 64 ; RMN/Arnaudet D. et Lewandowski H. : p. 79, 98 ; RMN/Bernard Ph. : p. 52 ; RMN/Blot G. et Lewandowski H. : p. 37, 40-41 ; RMN/Blot G. : p. 6, 7, 18, 19, 20, 23, 26, 38, 39, 48, 55, 57, 59, 60, 67, 78, 79, 89, 92, 94, 96-97, 102, 104, 105, 106, 107, 111, 130, 142, 144, 148, 158-159, 162, 164, 169, 170, 190-191 ; RMN/Blot G. et Jean C. : p. 48, 49 ; RMN/Bréjat H. : p. 29, 30, 31, 33, 35, 36, 43, 45, 51, 62, 66, 85, 86, 87, 93, 119, 123, 125, 127, 138, 160, 163, 165, 166, 171, 172, 173, 174-175, 176, 177 ; RMN/Droits réservés : p. 6, 7 ; RMN/Jean C. et Marboeuf P. : p. 101 ; RMN/Lewandowski H. : p. 71, 83, 99 ; RMN/Michel Urtado : couverture ; RMN/Peter Willi : p. 63 ; © Château de Versailles/Manaï J.-M. : p. 26, 57, 70, 73, 74, 76, 77, 88, 90, 91, 94, 98, 102, 103, 108, 112, 126, 131, 132, 140, 148, 152, 154, 155, 161, 185 ; © Château de Versailles/Milet Ch. : p.136, 137, 178, 179, 184, 186, 187, 188-189

Achevé d'imprimer par les Presses de Bretagne
le 20 mars 2008
Dépôt légal : avril 2008